LIVES OF GREAT RELIGIOUS BOOKS

The *Dead Sea Scrolls*

LIVES OF GREAT RELIGIOUS BOOKS

The *Dead Sea Scrolls*

A BIOGRAPHY

John J. Collins

PRINCETON UNIVERSITY PRESS

Princeton and Oxford

Copyright © 2013 by Princeton University Press
Published by Princeton University Press, 41 William Street,
Princeton, New Jersey 08540
In the United Kingdom: Princeton University Press, 6 Oxford Street,
Woodstock, Oxfordshire OX20 1TW

press.princeton.edu

Jacket photograph: *The Dead Sea Scrolls—Fragments of the War of the
Sons of Light and the Sons of Darkness*. Scroll found in Qumran Cave
No. 1, Israel. Photograph by Z. Radovan / Bible Land Pictures.

Library of Congress Cataloging-in-Publication Data

Collins, John Joseph, 1946–
    The Dead Sea scrolls : a biography / John J. Collins.
        pages cm — (Lives of great religious books)
    Includes bibliographical references and index.
    ISBN 978-0-691-14367-5 (hardcover)
    1. Dead Sea scrolls. I. Title.

British Library Cataloging-in-Publication Data is available

This book has been composed in Garamond Premier Pro

Printed on acid-free paper. ∞

Printed in the United States of America

10 9 8 7 6 5 4 3 2 1

CONTENTS

The Dead Sea Scrolls may seem to be an unlikely candidate for inclusion in a series on "biographies" of books.

The Scrolls are not in fact one book, but a miscellaneous collection of writings retrieved from caves near Qumran, at the northwest corner of the Dead Sea, between the years 1947 and 1956. In all, fragments of some nine hundred manuscripts were found. They are written mostly in Hebrew, with some in Aramaic and a small number in Greek. They date from the last two centuries BCE and the first century CE.

The collection is not entirely random, and much, though not all, of it seems to reflect the thought of a Jewish sect, usually identified as the Essenes, around the turn of the era. But the degree of coherence is controversial. While the Scrolls are often presumed to be the remnants of the library of a community that lived at the site of Qumran, this view seems increasingly unlikely. It is more likely that they were brought from several sectarian communities and hidden in the caves in the wilderness at the time of the Jewish Revolt against Rome (66–70 CE), although some presumably belonged to the community at the site. Unlike the Bible, which is also a collection of writings of diverse origin, the Scrolls were never known to constitute a distinct corpus in antiquity. Only after their accidental discovery in the middle of the twentieth century CE did the Scrolls become a corpus, or an entity that might be considered an appropriate subject for a "biography."

Moreover, the "biography" of these Scrolls is somewhat like that of Rip van Winkle. While other texts from antiquity influenced the Renaissance or the Reformation, the Scrolls just slept. What we have witnessed in the last sixty-five years or so is not so much a biography as a post-resurrection afterlife, separated from the original environment of the Scrolls by an interval of two millennia.

Nonetheless, the Scrolls now exist as a distinct corpus, with a life of its own. That life has several dimensions. The Scrolls are a scholarly resource, studied intensively by an expanding community of scholars, and of interest not only to historians of Judaism and Christianity but also to sociologists of religion and even philosophers. They are also a tourist attraction, in Jerusalem as well as in museum exhibitions throughout the Western world. Hundreds of thousands of people have waited patiently to catch a glimpse of selected illegible fragments in dimly lighted display cases and come away feeling that they have touched the past. In October 2011, when the Israel Museum launched a website featuring high-resolution photographs of five important Scrolls, the site got more than a million hits in the first week. Only a fraction of the people visiting the site are likely to have been scholars who could read the texts from the photographs. The Scrolls are fodder for the popular demand for "mysteries"—exotic, dimly understood lore that is paraded to stimulate curiosity in tabloid newspapers and television shows such as "Mysteries of the Bible." They are also sometimes a political symbol—testimony to the antiquity of Jewish roots in the land west of the Jordan, or conversely of modern Israeli expropriation of artifacts that were discovered in territory that was then under Jordanian control and whose ownership remains in dispute.

The Scrolls have been described as the greatest archeological discovery of the twentieth century. They have certainly been the most controversial.

The Scrolls attract popular interest, and also spark controversy, because they are primary documents from ancient Judea, from around the time of Jesus. Prior to the discovery of the Scrolls there were scarcely any Hebrew or Aramaic texts extant from that time and place. Inevitably, there has been an expectation, sometimes fevered, that these texts would shed light on Jesus or the movement of his followers. Several claims in this regard, beginning a few years after the discovery of the Scrolls and continuing into the twenty-first century, have been quite sensational, and it is precisely these claims that have attracted the attention of the wider public.

Controversy has been fanned by the fact that many of the fragmentary Scrolls remained unpublished for half a century. This delay has provided fertile ground for conspiracy theories, which were further nourished by the fact that several members of the official editorial team were Catholic priests—hence the suggestion that the Scrolls had been withheld from the public by order of the Vatican, because of the fear that they might undermine the historical credibility of Christianity. No serious scholars take such claims seriously, but they continue to stimulate suspicion and curiosity among the amateurs who flock to museum exhibits of the Scrolls.

Almost immediately after their discovery, a consensus developed that the Scrolls belonged to the (Jewish) sect of the Essenes, who had long been regarded as forerunners of Christianity. This consensus has aroused the wrath of dissenters to an extraordinary degree. The passion of the debate can hardly be explained by the ambiguities of the evidence. The same is true of the interpretation of the site of Qumran as an Essene settlement. At stake is the relevance of the Scrolls for mainline Jewish tradition, or the degree to which they should be taken to reflect a marginal form of Judaism, closer to Christianity than to the religion of the rabbis.

For a long time, the Scrolls were thought to be of greater interest to Christian scholars than to their Jewish counterparts. This impression was due in some part to the fact that no Jewish scholars were included in the editorial team, at the insistence of the Jordanian government. After the Arab-Israeli war of 1967, and the Israeli conquest of East Jerusalem where most of the Scrolls were housed, that picture began to change. When all the Scrolls became freely available in the 1990s, scholars who had been trained in rabbinic literature realized that there was plenty of material to interest them in the Scrolls. Consequently, the pendulum has swung from issues that were primarily of interest to Christian scholars to matters bearing on the distinctively Jewish character of the Scrolls and the continuity of the Scrolls with the later rabbinic tradition. Debates on all these issues have been heated, and have led to court proceedings in at least two cases—one involving the rights of editors of ancient texts and one involving attempts to defame a prominent scholar, as a way of advancing the views of a maverick in the field. These proceedings reflect a level of personal acrimony that is rare in the world of academic scholarship.

The story of the discovery of the Scrolls has often been told, and their contents have been amply described. There are also accounts, some of them self-serving, of "the battle for the scrolls," the controversies that led to the end of the monopoly of the editorial team and granting of access to any qualified scholar. The purpose of this volume is different.

Our purpose is to ask what difference the Scrolls have made to the study of ancient Judaism and early Christianity, and to probe what has been at stake in the debates that have often been so acrimonious. Are the Scrolls really worthy of all the attention they have received and continue to receive? Or are they only of curiosity value, as relics of an obscure and idiosyncratic sect that happened to live in the same time and place as Jesus of Nazareth? What is their enduring value likely to be?

For most of us who work in the field of biblical studies or ancient Judaism, these questions often seem unnecessary. Of course the Scrolls are of great historical value. In fields where new data rarely come to light, the Scrolls have seemed to be manna from heaven. They shed light on the two main religions of the Western world at a crucial time of transition for the one (Judaism) and the time of origin of the other (Christianity). In the case of Judaism, the Scrolls provide primary evidence for a period where it had been lacking. In the case of Christianity, the light is indirect, by illuminating the context in which Jesus and his earliest followers lived. This light is seldom of the sensational, headline-grabbing kind that popular writers on the Scrolls have repeatedly sought. But it is of fundamental importance for understanding the nature of Judaism and Christianity, and their tumultuous relationship over the centuries.

But are the Scrolls just something that God has provided for scholars to be busy with, as the book of Ecclesiastes might have suggested? It is unlikely that anyone's views about religion or life have been changed because of the discovery of the Scrolls. While the significance of the Scrolls lies mainly in the light they shed on ancient Judaism and early Christianity, the "biography" of the Scrolls is also an interesting study in the ethos of the scholarly community and modern media. The scholarly community is generally collegial and mutually supportive, but the Scrolls have brought to light some glaring exceptions that remind us that this community is no more free of original sin than any other segment of the human race. The story of the Scrolls also provides for an interesting study in the use, and manipulation, of scholarly data in the popular media. No doubt, the free press is one of the glories of democracy, but it can sometimes behave as indiscriminately as a hungry beast that only seeks whom it may devour.

The biography of the Scrolls, in short, touches on a range of interests that go beyond the historical value of the ancient texts. A major discovery like this shakes up the conventional world of scholarship in various ways, both on the level of ideas and on the level of human behavior. We will consider some of these ways in the following chapters.

The *Dead Sea Scrolls*

The Discovery of the Scrolls

On April 10, 1948, the Yale University News Bureau released an announcement, which appeared in the major newspapers of the English-speaking world in the following days:

> The earliest known manuscript of the entire biblical book of Isaiah from the Old Testament has been discovered in Palestine, it was announced today by Professor Millar Burrows of Yale University, the director of the American Schools of Oriental Research at Jerusalem.
>
> In addition, three other unpublished ancient Hebrew manuscripts have been brought to light by scholars in the Holy Land. Two of them have been identified and translated while the third still challenges recognition.
>
> The book of the prophet Isaiah was found in a well-preserved scroll of parchment. Dr. John C.

Trever, a Fellow of the School, examined it and recognized the similarity of the script to that of the Nash Papyrus – believed by many scholars to be the oldest known copy of any part of the Hebrew Bible.

The discovery is particularly significant since its origin is dated about the first century BC. Other complete texts of Isaiah are known to exist only as recently as the ninth century AD.

All these ancient scrolls, two in leather and the other in parchment, have been preserved for many centuries in the library of the Syrian Orthodox Monastery of St. Mark in Jerusalem. They were submitted to the American Schools of Oriental Research for study and identification by the Metropolitan Athanasius Yeshue Samuel and Father Butros Sowmy of the monastery.

Aside from the Book of Isaiah, a second scroll is part of a commentary on the Book of Habakkuk (Habakkuk is a Minor Prophet and this is one of the books of prophecy of the Old Testament), and a third appears to be the manual of discipline of a comparatively unknown little sect or monastic order, possibly the Essenes. The fourth manuscript is still unidentified.

The announcement went on to credit Dr. William H. Brownlee, a fellow at the American Schools, with the identification of the Habakkuk commentary, and to note that the Scrolls had been photographed, and were being studied further.

This was, in effect, the birth announcement of the Dead Sea Scrolls, although a small number of scholars were already aware of the discovery, and William F. Albright, the reigning authority on Hebrew paleography (and on many other matters relating to the ancient Near East) had already pronounced it "the greatest manuscript discovery of modern times." The announcement was inaccurate in one respect and incomplete in another.

First, these scrolls had not been preserved for many centuries in St. Mark's Monastery. They had been found in a cave near the Dead Sea, south of Jericho, by members of the Ta'amireh Bedouin tribe, some time in late 1946 or early 1947. Burrows claimed that the news release had been edited after it left his hands: what he had written was that the scrolls were acquired by the Syrian Orthodox Monastery of St. Mark. It is unclear whether someone deliberately changed the wording to conceal the true provenance of the fragments. The scrolls had indeed been brought to the American Schools by the Syrian Metropolitan, and it is conceivable that the editor assumed that they had been found in the monastery. In view of the intrigue surrounding the discovery, it is also quite conceivable that someone changed the wording deliberately. In fact, the Syrian archbishop on more than one occasion alleged that the scrolls were found in a monastery.

Second, the press release was misleading as to the number of scrolls that had been discovered, since not all of them had been brought to the attention of the American Schools. The initial discovery had been made by a Bedouin known as Mohammed ed-Dib ("the wolf") with at least one companion. This discovery involved three scrolls:

- a copy of the biblical book of Isaiah,
- a rule book for a community that was initially dubbed "the Manual of Discipline," and would later be called the Community Rule or referred to by its Hebrew name as *Serek ha-Yaḥad*, or as 1QS (i.e., the Serek from Qumran Cave 1), and
- a commentary, or *pesher*, on the biblical book of the prophet Habakkuk, relating the words of the prophet to events in the author's time, which was believed to be "the end of days."

Mohammed had brought them to Bethlehem in March 1947, and had shown them to antiquities dealers. Eventually, they were shown to Khalil Eskander Shahin, better known as Kando, a Syrian Orthodox merchant and cobbler from Bethlehem, apparently because the scrolls were written on leather. In April

1947, they were brought to the attention of Mar Athanasius Yeshue Samuel, the Syrian Orthodox Metropolitan, or Archbishop, at St. Mark's Monastery in the Old City in Jerusalem. The Metropolitan was aware of ancient reports that manuscripts had been found in a cave near Jericho, in a jar. One such report was attributed to Origen of Alexandria, who knew of a scroll that had been found "at Jericho in a jar" in the time of Antoninus, son of Severus, about 200 CE (Eusebius, *Ecclesiastical History* 6.16.4). Another, about 800 CE, was reported by Timotheus I, the Nestorian patriarch of Seleucia. In that case an Arab huntsman followed his dog into a cave and discovered books of the Old Testament, as well as others. The archbishop, then, had grounds to suspect that the scrolls were ancient and might be valuable.

In the meantime, in early summer 1947, four more scrolls were discovered by Bedouin, who brought them to the Syrian monastery but were turned away because of a misunderstanding. Three of these scrolls (a second Isaiah scroll, and previously unknown texts that became known as the War Scroll [1QM] and the Hodayot, or Thanksgiving Hymns [1QH]) were then sold to another antiquities dealer, Faidi Salahi. (The War Scroll was a manual for an apocalyptic battle between the Sons of Light and the Sons of Darkness. The Hodayot was a collection of hymns in a distinctive style, giving thanks to God for deliverance and exaltation.) The fourth scroll, later identified as the Genesis Apocryphon (a paraphrastic retelling of Genesis, in Aramaic), was acquired by Kando. In July 1947, Kando sold the original batch of scrolls to the Syrian Metropolitan. The three scrolls in Salahi's possession were brought to the attention of Eliezer Sukenik, a professor of archeology at the Hebrew University, in November of that year, just before the United Nations passed its resolution authorizing the creation of the state of Israel. Initially Sukenik had to peer at a fragment through a barbed wire fence. He asked his contact, an Armenian antiquities dealer, to bring some more samples. In the meantime, Sukenik got a pass to cross over to the zone where the dealer had his shop. After a brief examination, Sukenik was convinced that the fragments were genuine and decided to buy them for the Hebrew University. The initial purchase consisted of the Hodayot, or Thanksgiving Hymns, and the War Scroll. He thus became the first scholar to authenticate the scrolls. A little later he was able to purchase the second Isaiah scroll (1QIsaiah^b; 1Q designates scrolls found in Cave 1 near Qumran).

Mar Samuel, the Metropolitan, had also contacted Hebrew University a few months earlier. He told the people sent by the University that the manuscripts had been lying in the library of a monastery near the Dead Sea. They were not impressed, and recommended that he consult an expert in Samaritan studies. In January 1948, Kando's scrolls were shown to Sukenik by a member of the Syrian Orthodox community, Anton Kiraz, who had entered into a partnership with Mar Samuel. In this case, however, no purchase was negotiated. The Syrians decided to wait until the hostilities between Jews and Arabs subsided, and try to get an independent assessment of the value of the scrolls.

Only in February 1948 did the Syrians approach the American School of Oriental Research. The director, Millar Burrows, was away on a trip to Iraq, and John C. Trever, a recent PhD who had studied with Burrows at Yale, was in charge in his absence. There was also another young Fellow of the School in residence, William Brownlee. Trever was initially told that the scrolls were found in St. Mark's monastery. The Syrian emissary, Butros Sowmy, returned by taxi, carrying in his briefcase the great Isaiah scroll, the Manual of Discipline, the Commentary on Habakkuk and the Genesis Apocryphon. Trever, who pursued photography as a hobby, managed to persuade the Syrians to allow him to photograph the scrolls. Trever recognized the similarity of the script to that of the Nash Papyrus, a sheet of papyrus containing the Ten Commandments and the Shema (Deuteronomy 6:4–5: "Hear, O Israel") in Hebrew, that had been acquired from an Egyptian dealer and published in 1903, and had been dated to the second century BCE. Trever promptly sent sample photographs to Albright, expressing his belief that the Isaiah scroll was the oldest Bible document yet discovered. Albright promptly dated the script of the Isaiah scroll to the second century BCE, and wrote to Trever, congratulating him on the discovery. The Syrians now disclosed to Trever what they knew about the provenance of the scrolls, and also mentioned that they had some communications with Professor Sukenik. The Americans, however, did not know that Sukenik had already seen the manuscripts, or that he had other manuscripts from the same find. Sukenik disclosed his own knowledge of the scrolls in a press release of April 26, 1948. Descriptions of the scrolls were published in the September 1948 issue of the *Biblical Archaeologist* and in the October 1948 issue of the *Bulletin of the American Schools of Oriental Research*. Sukenik also published in Hebrew a preliminary survey of the scrolls he had acquired.

Eventually, the scrolls that had been acquired by the Syrian Metropolitan would also find their way into Israeli hands. Mar Samuel took them to America in January 1949, and continued to seek a buyer. In the polarized situation that followed the partition of Palestine, he did not want to sell them to a Jew. Moreover, the legal ownership of the scrolls had not been established, and the Jordanians considered him a smuggler. In June 1954, an advertisement was placed in the *Wall Street Journal*, under the heading "Miscellaneous for Sale":

> "*The Four Dead Sea Scrolls.*"
> Biblical Manuscripts, dating back to at least 200 BC, are for sale. This would be an ideal gift to an educational or religious institution by an individual or group.
> Box F 206, *The Wall Street Journal*.

This led to the purchase of the four scrolls for $250,000, by a banker named Sidney Esteridge. Unknown to the archbishop, Esteridge was acting on behalf of Sukenik's son, Yigael Yadin, who was lecturing in the United States at the time. Sukenik himself had died the previous year. Thus, the original "Dead Sea Scrolls" were reunited in Jerusalem, where a special building of the Israel Museum, The Shrine of the Book, was built to house them, in 1965.

Enter the Archeologists

Further fragmentary manuscripts from Qumran Cave 1 came to light in the course of 1948, including fragments of the Book of Daniel, 1 Enoch (an apocalyptic text known in full only in Ethiopic), and a scroll of prayers. The Jordanian Department of Antiquities decided that it was time to excavate the cave, which was identified by soldiers of the Arab legion in January 1949. The first excavation, in February–March 1949, was a joint project of the Palestine Archaeological Museum, the École Biblique, and the American School of Oriental Research. It was led by Roland de Vaux, a French Dominican priest based at the École, and overseen by Gerald Lankester Harding, an Englishman who was in charge of the Department of Antiquities of Jordan. They identified fragments of about seventy documents, including fragments of two of the original seven. There were also pottery shards and scraps of linen. The main items of value in the cave had already been recovered by the Bedouin.

The cave in question, known as Cave 1, is about three-quarters of a mile north of the ruins of Khirbet Qumran, which is itself a little less than a mile west of the Dead Sea, near its northern end. It was not immediately obvious that the scrolls were related to the ruins. Only at the end of 1951 were soundings made at the site. These brought to light pottery that was identical with what had been discovered in Cave 1, and also coins that established the approximate date. At that point de Vaux undertook a complete excavation of the ruins, and this was continued in four additional campaigns from 1953 to 1956.

The major scroll discoveries, however, were a result of the activities of the Bedouin. In the fall of 1951, they discovered scrolls in the caves of Wadi Murabbaʿat, far to the southwest of the first cave. De Vaux and Harding investigated, and found fragments of Greek, Hebrew, and Aramaic texts, as well as cloth, ropes, and baskets. These included letters of Simeon ben Kosibah, Prince of Israel, better known as Bar Kochba, who led the last Jewish revolt against the Romans in 132 CE, and also marriage contracts. These texts are not related to those found near Qumran, and are not usually included in the Dead Sea Scrolls, but they are of enormous importance for Jewish history. Murabbaʿat also yielded an important scroll of the Minor Prophets, but this was not discovered until 1955. A Greek scroll of the Minor Prophets was recovered from another location, Naḥal Ḥever, in summer 1952.

While the archeologists were busy with Wadi Murabbaʿat, the Bedouin returned to Qumran. In February 1952, they discovered manuscript fragments in a cave a few hundred yards south of Cave 1, which became known as Cave 2. This led to a systematic exploration of the cliffs above Qumran by the archeologists. Much pottery and some evidence of tents or shelters was discovered, but only one new cave, more than a mile north of the ruins, produced written material. This was Cave 3, which yielded the

Copper Scroll: two oxidized rolls of beaten copper on which text was inscribed. This scroll proved difficult to open. Eventually—in 1956—it was cut into small strips at the University of Manchester. Even before that, however, scholars had gotten an impression of its contents from the reverse impressions of the letters visible on the exterior. It appeared to contain a list of treasures and their hiding places.

As spring 1952 advanced, the archeologists again withdrew from Qumran, and the Bedouin returned to the scene. The ruins at Qumran sit on top of a marl terrace, and to this terrace the treasure hunters now turned their attention. In late summer 1952, they discovered a cave on the edge of the terrace, less than 200 yards from the ruins. This cave became known as Cave 4, and it contained fragments of hundreds of manuscripts. De Vaux and Harding promptly returned and excavated Cave 4 during September 1952. While the Bedouin had already removed many of the fragments, the archeologists discovered a small underground chamber that contained fragments of about one hundred different manuscripts. De Vaux proceeded to excavate five more caves on the marl terrace, one of which, Cave 6, was also discovered by the Bedouin. Small numbers of manuscripts were recovered from these caves. The final scroll cave, Cave 11, was discovered by the Bedouin in February 1956. This was located near Cave 3, more than a mile north of Khirbet Qumran. Like Cave 1, this cave contained well-preserved scrolls. Several of these were taken by the Bedouin. Only a small number were recovered *in situ* by the archeologists. Eventually fragments of thirty-one manuscripts from Cave 11 would be published.

With the discovery of Cave 11, the bulk of the Dead Sea Scrolls had been brought to light. The Bedouin continued their searching, and several archeological investigations were undertaken in the Judean desert in the following years. Important discoveries were made in Naḥal Ṣe'elim (Wadi Seiyal) and Naḥal Ḥever, some of the latter relating to the Bar Kochba revolt. Papyri from Samaria, dating to the time of Alexander the Great, were discovered in Wadi Daliyeh, less than ten miles north of Jericho, in 1962. These discoveries, however, are peripheral to our present story. More relevant are some manuscripts discovered during the excavation of Masada by Yigael Yadin in 1963–65. These included fragments of biblical books, and also of the apocryphal book of Ben Sira. Most interesting was a manuscript of *The Songs of the Sabbath Sacrifice*, a mystical text about angelic liturgy, of which a copy was also found in Qumran Cave 4, and which is usually included in editions of the Dead Sea Scrolls.

Yadin was also responsible for the recovery of another major scroll. For several years in the 1960s he had attempted to negotiate with Kando for the purchase of a complete scroll whose contents were unknown. In June 1967, in the course of the Arab-Israeli war, the Israelis gained control of all Jerusalem and its suburbs as far south as Bethlehem. Yadin was personal military adviser to the prime minister of Israel. He and a small group of Israeli intelligence officers located Kando in Bethlehem, and after an interrogation that has been described as "unpleasant," they took possession of the scroll. This turned out to be the Temple Scroll, one of the largest and best preserved of the Dead Sea Scrolls. Yadin eventually agreed to a settlement with Kando of $105,000. Most of the sum was provided by an English industrialist, Leonard Wolfson.

One other important text that is usually included with the Scrolls had been known for a half century before the discoveries of 1947. Two copies of it were found in the trove of material taken from the Geniza or storeroom of the Ben Ezra synagogue in Cairo in 1896, and published in 1910, under the title *Fragments of a Zadokite Work*, by Solomon Schechter, a Moldavian-born rabbi who had served on faculties at Cambridge and London, and was the second president of the Jewish Theological

Seminary in New York from 1902 to 1915. This document referred to "a new covenant in the land of Damascus" and to its members as "sons of Zadok." Hence Schechter dubbed it a Zadokite work. Later, it came to be known as "the Damascus Document" or CD (Cairo Damascus). Schechter observed that the annals of Jewish history contained no record of a sect agreeing in all points with the one depicted. When the first Dead Sea Scrolls were made public, however, it was immediately apparent that there was some relationship between them and the so-called Damascus Document. The "sons of Zadok" also figure prominently in the Manual of Discipline or Community Rule. A figure called the "Teacher of Righteousness," who played an authoritative role in the early history of the sect, appears both in the Document and in the commentary on Habakkuk, as does one of his adversaries, the "Man of the Lie." The relationship between the Damascus Document and the Qumran scrolls was subsequently confirmed when fragments of the Damascus Rule were found in Qumran Cave 4, but it was established before Cave 4 was discovered at all. How this document found its way to Cairo in the Middle Ages is not clear. Perhaps it was one of the texts that had been found in a cave near Jericho around 800 CE, as reported by Timotheus of Seleucia.

The Task of Publication

If the Dead Sea Scrolls had consisted only of the manuscripts found in Cave 1 and the Damascus Document, their story would have been quickly told. Facsimiles of the great Isaiah scroll and the Habakkuk commentary were published by the American School of Oriental Research in 1950, and the Manual of Discipline the following year. Sukenik published extracts of his texts already in 1948, and at the time of his death in 1953 had prepared full transcriptions, which were published, with plates, posthumously. The French scholar André Dupont-Sommer published a book-length study of the scrolls already in 1950. By the mid-1950s, detailed analyses had begun to appear, based mainly on the texts that were available by 1950. These texts were well preserved, easy to read, and promptly published. The trove of fragments recovered from Cave 4, however, was an entirely different matter. Here was a huge quantity of fragments, in an advanced state of decay. In the words of Frank Moore Cross, who was involved in the editorial process from an early point: "Many fragments are so brittle or friable that they can scarcely even be touched with a camel's-hair brush. Most are warped, crinkled, or shrunken, crusted with soil chemicals, blackened by moisture and age. The problems of cleaning, flattening, identifying, and piecing them together are formidable."[1]

Over 1953–54, an international team of scholars was assembled to work on editing the scrolls, under the leadership of de Vaux. Two Catholic priests—a Dominican Dominique Barthélemy and the Polish scholar Józef T. Milik—had already been enlisted by de Vaux to work on the materials from Cave 1 and Murabbaʿat. Barthélemy was already working at the École Biblique. Milik had studied in Rome at the Pontifical Biblical Institute, and had attracted de Vaux's attention because of his early articles on the Scrolls. Now the team's numbers increased. Another French priest, Jean Starcky, had served as a chaplain in the Allied forces during World War II, and was expert in Nabatean and Palmyrene studies. Several Protestant scholars were also recruited at this time. From England came John Allegro and John Strugnell. Allegro had served in the British navy during the war, after which he studied first at Manchester and then at Oxford. He was nominated to the Scrolls team by his Oxford professor, G. R. Driver. Driver also nominated Strugnell, who was only twenty-four when he set out for Jerusalem in 1954. Both Allegro and Strugnell will figure prominently in later chapters, for different reasons. Claus-Hunno Hunzinger, the sole German representative, was not trained in epigraphy and paleography, and eventually withdrew from the team. Frank Moore Cross, a brilliant student of W. F. Albright, was the first American member. He would go on to a distinguished career as Hancock Professor of Hebrew and Other Oriental Languages at Harvard (1958–92). His book, *The Ancient Library of Qumran and Modern Biblical Studies*, first published in 1958, remains one of the most influential accounts of the Scrolls. Another Catholic priest, Monsignor Patrick W. Skehan, from the Catholic University of America, joined the team in 1954. Skehan was not a prolific writer, but he enjoyed the respect of Albright, who invited him to serve as his substitute at Johns Hopkins when he was away. In 1958, another French priest, Maurice Baillet, was added. He had been a student at the École in 1952–54, and was well acquainted with the Scrolls. No Jewish scholars were included in the team, at the insistence of the Jordanian government, which had legal control over the Scrolls, since they had been found in Jordanian territory.

With funding from the Rockefeller Foundation, the members of the team were able to spend much of their time in Jerusalem, working on the Scrolls. This funding expired in 1960. By then, some of the team members had taken up teaching positions that would absorb much of their energy (Cross at Harvard, Strugnell at Duke). The work of assembling and identifying the fragments had been largely completed by that time, and the results were recorded in a concordance, compiled with the assistance of scholars who were not part of the official editorial team—Raymond Brown, Joseph Fitzmyer, Will Oxtoby, and Javier Teixidor. Brown and Fitzmyer, both Catholic priests, had studied with Albright, and would become the leading Catholic New Testament scholars of their generation, and Fitzmyer especially had a distinguished career as a Scrolls scholar. He would eventually be included in the editorial team some forty years after he had worked on the concordance.

The achievement of sorting the fragments and piecing the texts together should not be underestimated. Fragments of some nine hundred manuscripts were distinguished in the material taken from the caves around Qumran. The series established for the official publication, *Discoveries in the Judaean Desert*, or *DJD*, would eventually run to more than forty large volumes, and some important manuscripts, including several of the first ones discovered, were published outside the series. Many texts were published in articles in the 1950s and 1960s, but the pace of the official final publication was frustratingly slow. The first volume of the *DJD* series, containing materials from Cave 1, appeared in 1955. Four volumes appeared in the 1960s, including the first volume of Cave 4 materials, edited by John Allegro. De Vaux died suddenly in September 1971, and was replaced as general editor by Pierre Benoit O.P., who was a New Testament scholar rather than a specialist in the Scrolls. Only two volumes appeared during Benoit's term as editor, in 1977 and 1982. He retired in 1984, and died in 1987 at the age of eighty-one. In 1985, John Strugnell became editor-in-chief. By the end of the 1980s there was a furious clamor for the publication of the remaining scrolls, and eventually in 1990, Strugnell was replaced by Emanuel Tov, a well-respected text-critical scholar at the Hebrew University who had studied with Cross at Harvard. Thereafter, the pace of publication was accelerated, and thirty-three volumes appeared in less than twenty years. The upheaval that led to Strugnell's replacement and the reorganization of the editorial team will concern us in a later chapter. For the present, it will be well to reflect on the nature of this huge corpus of manuscripts that had unexpectedly come to light in the decade 1946–1956.

A Library in the Wilderness?

The contents of this corpus were diverse. Every book of the Hebrew Bible except Esther was represented. (A fragment of Nehemiah only came to light years later, but Ezra and Nehemiah are commonly viewed as one book.) Fragments of previously known noncanonical books, such as 1 Enoch and Jubilees, were discovered. Some texts were clearly sectarian, most obviously the rule books (the so-called Manual of Discipline or Community Rule and the Damascus Document) but also other texts such as the *Pesharim*, which were commentaries that related the prophetic books to the history of sect, the Hodayot or Thanksgiving Hymns, and the War Scroll. Other texts were not conspicuously sectarian. Several could be described as "parabiblical"—they are related in some way to the canonical books, but are independent compositions. The Genesis Apocryphon, an Aramaic re-telling of stories from Genesis, which was discovered in Cave 1 but not immediately identified, is a case in point. There are texts concerned with the cultic calendar and with religious law, poetic and liturgical texts, wisdom texts, and eschatological texts. There are also narrative texts, such as the fragmentary "tales from the Persian court" (4Q550). A few fragments appear to recall historical events by mentioning names and events (4Q331–3; 468e). Only a handful of texts appear to contain records or accounts of commercial transactions. There are a few exorcisms and magical texts, and some texts written in cryptic script (later deciphered).

Since the initial batch of scrolls included a rule for a sectarian religious community, the immediate assumption was that the scrolls had been the property of that community and were hidden for safekeeping in time of upheaval. This assumption appeared to be confirmed by the excavation at Qumran and the discovery of Cave 4, a mere stone's throw from the site. While no manuscripts were actually found in the ruins, the archeologists found pottery identical to that in Cave 1. Consequently, the corpus of texts recovered from the caves became known as "the library of Qumran," a designation popularized by Frank Moore Cross in his classic account of the scrolls in 1958.[2]

The designation of the corpus as a library was not usually accompanied by much reflection about what it might mean to have such a huge library at a location in the wilderness. There was some speculation about the preparation and use of the manuscripts. A room in the ruined site was identified as a *scriptorium*, by analogy with medieval monasteries. The influential German scholar, Hartmut Stegemann, writing in the 1990s, estimated that the supposed library had contained about a thousand scrolls, and tried to distinguish between those that were in constant use and those that were in little demand.[3] Emanuel Tov has argued that there was a distinctive "Qumran scribal practice," which is attested in a group of 167 texts, biblical and nonbiblical, which exhibit distinctive orthography and morphology.[4] These include most of the texts commonly identified as sectarian, but there are exceptions. According to Stegemann, this library was the main basis of the economic existence of the community and the principal locus of their educational opportunities and studies.

Nonetheless, the idea of a library of this size by the shores of the Dead Sea is anomalous. Libraries were rare in antiquity, although they became somewhat more common in the Hellenistic period. The great palace library of the Assyrian king Asshurbanipal and the famous library of Alexandria were exceptional, and Qumran was a far cry from Alexandria. Libraries were often associated with temples, but these were usually of modest size. The largest known Mesopotamian temple library had about eight hundred tablets. At the other end of the spectrum, a temple at Edfu in Hellenistic Egypt had a catalogue with merely thirty-five titles. If indeed the site of Qumran housed a community such as the one described in the "Manual of Discipline" or Community Rule (1QS), then we should expect that there was some library at the site, since the members were supposed to devote a part of their nights to study (1QS 6:6–7). But it is difficult to believe that a community at this remote location had a library equal to that of the largest Mesopotamian temples.

In the early 1960s, a German scholar, Karl-Heinrich Rengstorff, suggested that the scrolls were the library of the Jerusalem temple.[5] He supposed that the library had been taken out of Jerusalem and hidden in the wilderness in 68 CE, when the priests realized that Jerusalem was doomed. So they smuggled out a great quantity of gold and silver, now documented in the Copper Scroll, and a library with archives in which the tradition and the spiritual life of Judaism since the time of Nehemiah were preserved. This action, argued Rengstorff, showed their good sense in realizing that books rather than the temple would ensure the future of Judaism.

The idea that the Copper Scroll documented actual treasures that had been hidden for safekeeping had been put forward by another German scholar, Karl-Georg Kuhn in 1954, before the scroll had even been unrolled.[6] Kuhn originally supposed that the treasure was that of the Qumran community. Later, when the scroll was unrolled and fully legible, he changed his mind, and supposed that so great a treasure could only have come from the Jerusalem temple. The scroll contains a list of sixty-four deposits of treasure, some two hundred tons of gold and silver, and also incense and other valuable substances. These were hidden all over the countryside, but were concentrated especially in the region surrounding Jerusalem and the temple. There was an acrimonious dispute about the Copper Scroll between members of the editorial team in the late 1950s. John Allegro accepted the reality of the treasures, assuming at first that they came from the community but then agreeing with Kuhn and others who suggested that the temple was the source. In contrast, J. T. Milik thought the scroll was an example of folklore, and de Vaux allegedly dismissed it as the "whimsical product of a deranged mind."[7] Since the scroll is inscribed in copper, however, and is in a dry, documentary style, later scholarship has dismissed Milik's "folklore" theory. Whether a sectarian movement could have amassed such wealth by collecting but withholding temple offerings is uncertain. Cave 3, where the Copper Scroll was found, is the cave farthest from the ruins of Qumran, and it may have been deposited independently.

But the idea that the scrolls came from the Jerusalem temple is also problematic. To begin with, the temple library is not well attested, although it is probably safe to assume that one existed. According to 2 Maccabees 2:13–15, Nehemiah was believed to have "founded a library and collected the books about the kings and prophets, and the writings of David, and letters of kings about votive offerings." (No such activity is reported in the biblical book of Nehemiah.) Likewise Judas Maccabee was said to have collected all the books that had been lost on account of the war. There are scattered references in the historical writings of Josephus to books laid up in the temple. The historian says that Titus allowed him to take some sacred books when the temple was destroyed, and the spoils taken by the Romans are known to have included a copy of the Jewish Law (Josephus, *Jewish War* 7.150), which was laid up in Rome in the Temple of Peace (*Jewish War* 7.162). Josephus claims that the records of the Jewish people were kept by the chief priests and the prophets, who ensured their authenticity, but he also says that the number of "justly accredited books" was only twenty-two (Josephus, *Against Apion*, 1.31). Some scholars believe that the books that were laid up in the temple became what we know as the canon of Hebrew scriptures. All this suggests that the library in the Jerusalem temple was quite modest in size.

Even more problematic for the temple hypothesis is the fact that so many of the scrolls are clearly sectarian in character, and are highly critical of the Jerusalem temple and the High Priesthood. There are eleven copies of the sectarian Community Rule, seven copies of the Damascus Rule, and six copies of an avowedly separatist halachic document known as 4QMMT, "Some of the Works of the Torah," which sets out the issues on which this sect disagreed with other Jews. The archenemy of the Teacher in the *Pesharim*, or biblical commentaries, is the Wicked Priest, who is universally understood to have been a High Priest. In contrast, only one text 4Q448, which has been interpreted as a prayer for "Jonathan the King" (probably the Hasmonean king Alexander Jannaeus) can be construed as positive to the Hasmonean priest-kings, and even that is disputed. It is incomprehensible that the Jerusalem temple would have contained such an archive of sectarian writings, critical of the temple.

Norman Golb, long-time professor at the University of Chicago, who became the most avid defender of the "Jerusalem hypothesis," sought to get around this problem by supposing that the scrolls came from various libraries in Jerusalem. But this is still problematic. It does not explain the high number of sectarian writings, or the lack of writings sympathetic to the Jerusalem priesthood. Neither does it explain the absence of any writings that could be construed as Pharisaic. Golb has made much of the absence of documentary writings (financial records and the like) from among the scrolls. He reconciles this with his Jerusalem hypothesis by recalling that the official archives in Jerusalem were burned by the insurgents in 66 CE, at the beginning of the war against Rome (Josephus, *Jewish War* 2.427). But if the scrolls came not only from the Jerusalem temple, but also from private libraries, we should still expect that some archival material would be preserved, as it was in the Bar Kochba period. Conversely, archival material at Qumran may have perished when the settlement was burned down by the Romans. The paucity of documentary material in the scrolls is surprising in any case, but it lends no support to the theory of Jerusalem provenance.

Nonetheless, the idea that all this material came from the library of one small settlement remains difficult. Golb made a valid observation that the number of scribal hands detected in the scrolls was far greater than one would expect if they had all been produced at a small settlement. Moreover, some manuscripts were clearly older than the settlement at Qumran, so it was evident that they had been brought from elsewhere.

Golb supposed that the inhabitants of the site had merely supplied pots for hiding the scrolls. Yet, in view of the sheer proximity of Cave 4 to the ruins, it is hard to believe that the scrolls did not have a more significant association with the site. Moreover, while the corpus includes a wide range of materials, it nonetheless seems to exclude certain kinds of literature, such as the books of the Maccabees. It is not a random collection, but has a sectarian character.

My own suggestion on the provenance of the scrolls is bound up with my understanding of the sectarian movement attested in the rule books. Too often, "the Qumran Community" has been regarded by scholars as an isolated, self-sufficient community, cut off from the outside world. But both the Community Rule and the Damascus Document envision multiple settlements within the same broad movement. The Community Rule speaks of a quorum of ten members for an assembly (1QS 6:3, 6). The Damascus Document speaks of people who live in "camps" according to the order of the land (CD 7:6). The movement is commonly identified with the Essenes, and these too are said to have been spread throughout the land.

The corpus of scrolls found near Qumran has a sectarian character, but is too large and diverse to have been the library of a single settlement. I suggest that these scrolls represent many libraries, but sectarian libraries; the libraries of many settlements of the sect or movement. At the time of the war against Rome, members of the sect from various communities fled to the wilderness, and sought refuge with their brethren, either because of the remoteness of the area or because Qumran was a "motherhouse" as some have proposed. They would have brought their scrolls with them. Hence the multiplicity of rules with minor variations, and the great variety of scribes attested by the handwriting. On this scenario, the scrolls would include the library of the people who lived at Qumran, but also the libraries of many *sectarian* communities that lived elsewhere. Both the sectarian character of the corpus and its internal variety can thus be acknowledged.

Almost from the time of the first discovery, the sectarian movement in question has been identified with the sect of the Essenes, an identification that eventually became a matter of heated controversy.

We shall turn to the Essenes in the following chapter.

Further Reading

The story of the discovery of the Scrolls, and the composition of the editorial team, are described in great detail by Weston W. Fields, *The Dead Sea Scrolls. A Full History* Volume 1 (Leiden: Brill, 2009).

For the roles of Eliezer Sukenik and Yigael Yadin, see Neil Asher Silberman, *A Prophet from Amongst You. The Life of Yigael Yadin: Soldier, Scholar, and Mythmaker of Modern Israel* (Reading, MA: Addison-Wesley, 1993). (On the acquisition of the Temple Scroll, see pp. 304–11.)

On the Cairo Geniza and Solomon Schechter, see Adina Hoffman and Peter Cole, *Sacred Trash: The Lost and Found World of the Cairo Geniza* (New York: Schocken, 2011).

A full inventory of the Scrolls is provided by Emanuel Tov, in collaboration with S. J. Pfann, "List of the Texts from the Judaean Desert," in Tov et al., *The Texts from the Judaean Desert* (DJD 39; Oxford: Clarendon, 2002), 27–114. For an attempt to organize the material by genre, loosely defined, see Armin Lange with Ulrike Mittmann-Richert, "Annotated List of the Texts from the Judaean Desert Classified by Content and Genre," in Tov et al., *The Texts from the Judaean Desert*, 115–64. Tov's theory of a distinctive Qumranic scribal practice can be found in his book, *Scribal Practices and Approaches Reflected in the Texts Found in the Judean Desert* (STDJ 54; Leiden: Brill, 2004), 261–88.

Classic statements of the consensus view of the Scrolls and their provenance can be found in Frank Moore Cross, *The Ancient Library of Qumran and Modern Biblical Studies* (3rd ed.; Sheffield: Sheffield Academic Press, 1995, originally published by Doubleday in 1958), J. T. Milik, *Ten Years of Discovery in the Wilderness of Judaea* (Studies in Biblical Theology 26; London: SCM, 1959) and Geza Vermes, *The Dead Sea Scrolls. Qumran in Perspective* (Philadelphia: Fortress, 1977).

The theory that the Scrolls were brought from Jerusalem and hidden in the caves is expounded by K.-H. Rengstorff, *Hirbet Qumran and the Prob-

lem of the Dead Sea Cave Scrolls (Leiden: Brill, 1963), and Norman Golb, *Who Wrote the Dead Sea Scrolls? The Search for the Secret of Qumran* (New York: Scribner, 1995).

For the author's views on the nature of the sectarian movement and the provenance on the Scrolls, see John J. Collins, *Beyond the Qumran Community. The Sectarian Movement of the Dead Sea Scrolls* (Grand Rapids: Eerdmans, 2010).

Five of the major Scrolls can now be viewed online at http:dss.collections.imj.org.il/: the Great Isaiah Scroll, the Temple Scroll, the War Scroll, the Pesher or Commentary on Habakkuk, and the Community Rule or Manual of Discipline.

The Essenes

Almost immediately after the discovery of the Dead Sea Scrolls in 1947, several people concluded independently that they were writings of the Jewish sect of the Essenes, who were described by Philo and Josephus, and briefly by the Roman writer Pliny the Elder. In February 1948, one Ibrahim Sowmy, whose brother was an assistant of the Syrian metropolitan, Mar Samuel, remarked to John Trever that he knew of a group called "Essenes" who lived near the Dead Sea in the first century, and suggested that the Scrolls might have belonged to them.[1] The report that Essenes lived near the Dead Sea was derived from the notice of Pliny, and this seems to have been the first consideration that prompted their association with the Scrolls. In the announcement issued by Yale University in April 1948, Millar Burrows referred to "the manual of discipline of a comparatively unknown little sect or monastic order, possibly the Essenes." Burrows did not explain his reasoning here, but the reference to a "manual of discipline" suggests that he was impressed by the similarities between the text later known as *Serek ha-Yahad*, or the Community Rule, and the description of Essene community life in Josephus. On October 3, 1948, the Hebrew newspaper *Davar* carried an article with the headline: "Discovery last year of Genizah from Judaean Wilderness," announcing the imminent publication of the first scholarly book on the Scrolls by Eliezer Sukenik. After a brief account of the find, the article commented: "It is not yet clear who the owners of this storehouse were. However, the contents of one scroll, which is a book of regulations for conduct of the members of a society or sect, have enabled Professor Sukenik to suggest that the documents belong to the sect of Essenes, who, according to ancient literary sources, dwelled on the western side of the Dead Sea in the vicinity of En-Gedi."[2] It is not clear exactly when Sukenik reached this conclusion. His son, Yigael Yadin, claimed that his father was the first to suggest the identification with the Essenes, and this claim is endorsed by Neil Asher Silberman, who writes: "The Essene identification seemingly was confirmed when, in March 1948, Sukenik had the opportunity to examine the four additional scrolls," including the so-called

CHAPTER 2

Manual of Discipline.[3] In any case, the identification appears to have occurred independently to several people.

The Ancient Accounts of the Essenes

The Essenes had long been something of an enigma in the context of ancient Judaism. They are never mentioned explicitly in Hebrew or Aramaic sources, and they are absent from the New Testament. They are known from a small number of Greek and Latin authors, of whom the most important are Philo of Alexandria, Josephus, and Pliny the Elder.

Philo, who calls them Essaeans, says that they were exceptionally virtuous people, who lived in villages. They refrained from animal sacrifices and avoided cities. They lived "without goods or property," but had all things in common. They had common meals, and whatever belonged to each belonged to all. They had no implements of war, and they rejected slavery. They had no time for philosophy, since it did not lead to the acquisition of virtue, but devoted themselves to the study of ethics, by studying the ancestral laws, especially on the seventh day, when they met in synagogues (*Quod omnis probus liber sit*, 75–91). Moreover, "shrewdly providing against the sole or principal obstacle threatening to dissolve the bonds of communal life, they banned marriage at the same time as they ordered the practice of perfect continence. Indeed, no Essaean takes a woman because women are selfish, excessively jealous, skillful in ensnaring the morals of a spouse and in seducing him by endless charms" (*Apologia pro Iudaeis*, quoted by Eusebius, *Praeparatio Evangelica*, 8:6–7). They have no children or young men among them, because of their immaturity, but they are "men of ripe years inclining to old age" (*Apologia*, 3).

Josephus gives a much more detailed description in *Jewish War* (*JW*) 2.119–61, and also gives a shorter account in *Antiquities* 18.18–22. He ranks the Essenes as the third of three Jewish schools of philosophy, after the Pharisees and Sadducees. They renounce pleasure as an evil and regard continence as a virtue. Like Philo, Josephus says that they reject marriage, but unlike Philo he claims that they adopt the children of others at a tender age. According to Josephus, "it is not that they abolish marriage, or the propagation of the species resulting from it, but they are on their guard against the licentiousness of women and are convinced that none of them is faithful to one man." At the end of his main account of the Essenes in *JW*, however, Josephus adds that "there exists another order of Essenes, who although in agreement with the others on the way of life, usages and customs, are separated from them on the subject of marriage," out of concern for the propagation of the species. Nonetheless, they restrict their sexual intercourse and do not engage in it when their wives are pregnant, "thereby showing that they do not marry for pleasure but because it is necessary to have children."

Josephus describes the common life of the sect in greater detail than does Philo. He also emphasizes that the Essenes are not restricted to one town but "in every town several of them form a colony." They live a peaceful, simple life, and have their possessions in common. They do nothing unless ordered by the superiors. Before sunrise, they recite ancestral prayers to the sun, as if entreating it to rise. When they assemble for meals, they bathe in cold water to purify themselves. Purity is required for entry into the refectory. A priest recites prayers before and after meals. In *Ant* 18, Josephus tells us further that priests prepare the bread and food. The Essenes "send offerings to the temple but perform their sacrifices using different customary purifications. For this reason, they are barred from entering into the common enclosure, but offer sacrifice among themselves."

Especially noteworthy is the elaborate process of admission, which is gradual, over a period of three years. First there is a probationary year when they must prove their continence. After this they are admitted to the purificatory baths at a higher degree. Only after two further years are they fully admitted to the community and allowed to partake of the common food. Those who are admitted swear to transmit none of the doctrines except as they have received them, and "to preserve the books of their sect and the names of the angels" (*JW* 2.142). Those who are expelled from the sect suffer a miserable death, for they are bound by oaths and customs that forbid them to share the food of others.

Josephus attributes to the Essenes the gift of prophecy: "There are some among them who, trained as they are in the study of the holy books and the different sorts of purifications, and the sayings of the prophets, become expert in foreseeing the future: they are rarely deceived in their predictions" (*JW* 2.159). He illustrates their predictive ability by a number of anecdotes.

According to Josephus, the Essenes believed in the immortality of the soul, and reward and punishment after death. (The early Christian writer, Hippolytus, in contrast, attributes to them a belief in bodily resurrection.) In the *Antiquities*, he says that they followed the way of life revealed to the Greeks by Pythagoras (*Ant* 15.371). This statement has intrigued modern scholars, who have often speculated on whether they might have been influenced by the Pythagoreans. Another remark of Josephus is more enigmatic. He says that they "live in no way different from, but as much as possible like, the so-called majority of the Dacians" (*Ant* 18:22). The Dacians lived to the east of the Black Sea, and it is not clear how they resembled the Essenes. It is apparent, however, that Josephus wrote for Greek readers and was trying to explain the Essenes by analogies that his readers might understand.

The much shorter notice by Pliny the Elder, in his *Natural History* 5.17.4 (73), affirms that the Essenes are "a people (*gens*) unique of its kind . . . without women and renouncing love entirely, without money, and having for company only the palm trees. He marvels that this celibate community had managed to renew itself "for thousands of centuries." Unlike Philo and Josephus, Pliny seems to know only one Essene settlement, to the west of the Dead Sea, where they "have put the necessary distance between themselves and the insalubrious shore." "Below them" (*infra hos*) was En-Gedi. Pliny's account is geographical in focus: he is concerned with the Essenes only insofar as they lived in proximity to the Dead Sea. His account does not necessarily preclude the existence of other settlements. He wrote after the Jewish War, when Jerusalem and En-Gedi were in ruins, but he gives no indication that the Essene settlement had been disrupted. The association of the Essenes with the area around the Dead Sea would loom large in attempts to identify the people responsible for the Dead Sea Scrolls.

Philo also writes of a group called the Therapeutae, whom he presents as a counterpart of the Essenes; while the latter are said to pursue the active life, the Therapeutae pursued the contemplative one. Hence the name of Philo's treatise, *On the Contemplative Life*. Like the Essenes, these were celibate, but they included women as well as men and were located not in Judea but in Egypt, near Alexandria. Philo describes them as pursuing a mystical life, which included a common meal, allegorical interpretation of scripture, and hymn singing. This group obviously resembles the Essenes, but the actual relationship has always been controversial.

Traditional Views of the Essenes

The Essenes had intrigued scholars long before the discovery of the Scrolls. Here was a supposedly Jewish sect that seemed far removed from rabbinic Judaism, and in some respects resembled Christianity, especially Christian monasticism, which did not arise until some centuries later. Long before the discovery of the Scrolls, discussions of the Essenes veered between two vantage points—one of which viewed them in relation to Christianity and the other of which tried to make sense of them in terms of rabbinic Judaism. To a great degree, the debates about the Essenes in the nineteenth century anticipate the debates about the Scrolls a century later.

For a long time, the Essenes were viewed through the lens of Christianity. Eusebius, the scholar and historian who became bishop of Caesarea in 314 CE, thought that the Therapeutae, whom he assumed to be a branch of the Essenes, were Christian ascetics (*Ecclesiastical History* 2.16). The idea that they were the first monks persisted into the Middle Ages. At the time of the Reformation, the Essenes/Therapeutae served as a proxy for debates about monasticism. Protestants argued that the Essenes were a Jewish group, and so the rise of monasticism represented a lapse back into Jewish ways. Catholics countered that the Therapeutae showed the existence of monasticism in the earliest stages of the Christian movement, and could cite the testimony of the Church Fathers in support. In the heat of the debate, even Jesus, the apostles, and John the Baptist were alleged to be Essenes. The Christian character of the Therapeutae was firmly debunked by the great classical grammarian Joseph Justus Scaliger (1540–1609), although it was still maintained in Catholic and Anglican circles for some time later.

The period of the Enlightenment brought a new set of concerns to the fore. Jesus was now seen as a human being, whose thought was shaped by his environment. He was seen to share with the Essenes an ideal of brotherhood and distrust of riches, with little reliance on the temple. He was even thought to have spent his formative years in the Essene order. Essenism was now thought of as an environment in which a pacifistic, non-materialist spirituality might be nurtured. The philosopher Voltaire admired the Essenes, and the leading biblical scholar, J. D. Michaelis, saw affinities to Essenism in the Gospel of Luke. The Essenes were even proposed as progenitors of the Freemasons, as progressive thinkers, interested in universal morality. Needless to say, there was also significant opposition to such ideas. The deist Robert Taylor (1784–1844), who declared that "in every rational sense that can be attached to the word, they [Essenes] were the authors and real founders of Christianity,"[4] was imprisoned for blasphemy. (Admittedly, the charge was not based only on his views of the Essenes.)

The nineteenth century saw the rise of historical methods in the manner of von Ranke, and the attempt to free the study of history from dogmatic concerns. Scholars were increasingly aware of the differences between Jesus and the Essenes. The association of Jesus with the Essenes persisted, however, in popular Christian literature.

The Essenes and Judaism

Jewish scholars, however, were not willing to abandon the Essenes to Christianity. Already in the sixteenth century, the Jewish scholar Azariah de Rossi (1513/4–1577/8) was bothered by the lack of mention of the Essenes in the rabbinic corpus, and he suggested that they were in fact identical with the Boethusians, a group closely related to the Sadducees. Their Jewish character was thereby assured. Scholars of the *Wissenschaft des Judentums* ("scientific study of Judaism") movement in the nineteenth century, such as Zecharias Frankel, made a more influential suggestion. The Essenes should be associated with the Hasidim, or pious ones, who are mentioned in the books of Maccabees, but also in the rabbinic writings. These scholars were distrustful of the Greek and Latin accounts of the Essenes, and sought to integrate them into rabbinic tradition. Both the Pharisees and the Essenes were thought to have developed from the Hasidim. The dominant Jewish view of the Essenes in the mid-second century BCE was summed up well by Isaak Marcus Jost: "The Essenes are exactly the same that the other Rabbis wished to be who endeavoured to practise the Levitical law of purity, as leading to higher consecration. They have neither another creed nor another law, but simply institutions peculiar to this brotherhood . . . Their views and tenets are therefore also to be found in the utterances of the learned and the Rabbis who did not enter their order, so that they did not look upon the Essenes as opponents or apostates, but, on the contrary, as holding the same opinions with increased claims and some fewer enjoyments, whom many out of their own midst joined, and who were called Chassidim or Zenuim."[5] The view that Essenism was related to Pharisaism, insofar as both were concerned with strict purity, also won favor among Christian scholars. This strand of scholarship reached its apex in the work of Emil Schuerer, the great German historian of Judaism at the end of the nineteenth century, who declared that Essenism was "Pharisaism in the superlative."[6] Specifically Pharisaic were the strict observance of the law, and the anxiety about purity. The latter explains why the Essenes separated themselves from the rest of Judaism and formed their own organization. The rejection of sacrifice amplified the breach with their contemporaries. Schuerer allowed that some foreign influences may also have been at work, but the question was complicated by doubts about the trustworthiness of

Josephus, who may have imposed a Greek coloring on his account.

In the mid-nineteenth century, a new way was found to relate the Essenes to their Jewish context. The publication of the Ethiopic book of Enoch in 1821 had opened up a strand of Palestinian Judaism different from the Rabbis, and led to the recognition of apocalyptic literature as a genre. In 1853, Adolf Jellinek, an Austrian Jewish scholar, proposed that the Book of Enoch was a remnant of Essene literature. Adolf Hilgenfeld, a professor of New Testament and Christian history at Jena, related the asceticism of the Essenes more broadly to apocalyptic visionary practice. Fasting is a prelude to visionary experience in Daniel and Enoch, and in other apocalyptic writings. He even suggested that the name Essene was derived from the Aramaic word for "seers" (*chozin*). Hilgenfeld returned to the subject repeatedly in the course of a long career. He speculated about Persian, and even Buddhist, influence, although he eventually abandoned the latter idea. The idea that Essenism was related to the apocalyptic strand of Judaism, however, was endorsed by several scholars, who did not necessarily make it the primary factor in their account of the Essenes.

One of the scholars who affirmed continuity with the apocalyptic strand of Judaism was Ernest

Renan (1823–92), one of the leading French intellectuals of the nineteenth century. In his *Life of Jesus*, Renan wrote: "Essenism, which seems to have been directly related to the apocalyptic school . . . offered as it were a first rough sketch of the great discipline soon to be instituted for the education of mankind," by which he meant Christianity. Renan also wrote that most of the distinctive features of Essenism could be explained as exaggerations of orthodox Judaism. The rejection of sacrifices echoed the ancient prophets. The prudishness of the sect and its exaggerated ablutions were in the spirit of ancient Judaism, and of the Pharisees, but may also reflect some Persian influence. Here Renan thought of John the Baptist. Since the Pharisaic observance of the law rendered life impossible, the Essenes, like John the Baptist, withdrew to the wilderness. Renan accepted Schuerer's view that the Essenes were the superlative form of Pharisaism. His most famous pronouncement, however, was that "Christianity was an Essenism that survived." He doubted that there was direct contact between the early Christians and the Essenes, but he thought the similarities were profound, noting the common meal, community of goods, etc. Essenism represented an attempt to draw the moral consequences of Judaism and the preaching of the prophets. Pharisaism, according to Renan, failed because it was "reduced to the observance of the law." Essenism could not last, because of its extreme form of life, but it anticipated the Christian ideal of the meek who will inherit the earth. Renan's views would be recalled and invoked after the discovery of the Scrolls, in the course of the first great controversy about their relation to Christianity.

By the early twentieth century, the idea that the Essenes were either related or analogous to the Pharisees was well established. Often, both parties were thought to be descended from the Hasidim of the Maccabean period. Scholars who subscribed to this view included Jews and Christians, Catholics and Protestants. This supposed genealogy of the Essenes would loom large in reconstructions of the history of the sect that produced the Dead Sea Scrolls. Some of these scholars also attributed noncanonical books such as 1 Enoch and the Assumption of Moses to the Essenes.

Essenism as a Foreign Body

There was, however, a quite different way of understanding the Essenes, that was prompted by Josephus' own mention of the Pythagoreans. Pythagoras was a Greek philosopher from the sixth century BCE, who had founded a sect or society that bore his name. He was associated with the doctrine of the transmigration of souls, and was thought to have influenced Plato. He was said to have taught that friends should have all things in common, and his followers were said to have shared their possessions. They formed an exclusive society, greatly concerned with purity, and required an elaborate system of initiation over several years. There was also provision for expulsion from the community. Most of the sources about the Pythagorean way of life, however, date from the third century CE, whereas the community founded by Pythagoras had died out no later than the fourth century BCE. How far the accounts reflected the practice of actual Pythagorean communities is uncertain, but there was at least a literary tradition about the Pythagoreans in the Hellenistic period.

The idea that the Essenes were Jewish Pythagoreans was suggested already in the seventeenth century, and occasionally revived. Major figures who subscribed to the Pythagorean derivation of the Essenes in the nineteenth century included the great Tübingen New Testament scholar, F. C. Baur, in an essay on Apollonius of Tyana and the New Testament in 1832, and the historian of Greek philosophy, Eduard Zeller (1814–1908). Basic to both movements was the anthropological dualism of body and soul. Matter was inherently unclean. Animal sacrifice was unacceptable because of the defilement it entailed. The Pythagoreans were also said to have practiced community of property. Zeller remained to be persuaded that a movement characterized by sun worship, celibacy, and asceticism could be derived from traditional Judaism. The high point of speculation on Pythagorean influence came in the work of a Jewish scholar, Isidore Lévy. Writing in 1927, Lévy argued for wide-ranging Pythagorean influence on ancient Judaism, but found in the Essenes his prime example of a Jewish group modeled on the Neo-Pythagorean way of life, with its emphasis on asceticism and communal living.[7] Other syncretistic explanations of the Essenes were occasionally suggested, notably a derivation from Zoroastrianism, which was energetically defended by the English New Testament scholar, J. B. Lightfoot.[8]

A distinctive position was staked out by the great scholar of Hellenistic Judaism Moritz Friedländer (1844–1919).[9] Friedländer argued that to regard Essenism as intensified Pharisaism was to rob it of its inner core. In his view, the Essenes were Greek-speaking Jews, nourished by the kind of philosophical Hellenistic Judaism typified by Philo and the Therapeutae; hence their anthropological dualism of body and soul, and their repudiation of sacrifices. In short, much of what seemed "Pythagorean" to other interpreters was for Friedländer the Greek-speaking Judaism of Alexandria.

Underlying Motives in the Debate

It is now obvious that dogmatic interests were at stake in the discussion of the Essenes in the era of the Reformation, and again in the Enlightenment. In the earlier period, the idea that the Essenes were Christian was a way of affirming the antiquity, and therefore the authenticity, of Christianity. Later, in the more humanistic context of the Enlightenment, the suggestion that the Essenes anticipated key aspects of early Christianity was taken in some quarters to undermine the claim of supernatural revelation, and to show that Christianity was human, all too human. Both of these tendencies to impose ideological concerns on the discussion of the Essenes would persist in debates about the Dead Sea Scrolls in the second half of the twentieth century.

It may also be argued that the attempt to reclaim the Essenes for Judaism by assimilating them to the Pharisees sprang from dogmatic concerns. This was true of the systematic distrust of Philo and Josephus, and the attempt to identify references to the Essenes in the rabbinic corpus. In these cases, rabbinic Judaism was taken as authentic Judaism, and the Essenes had to be redeemed by their conformity to rabbinic interests. Conversely, one might suspect that dogmatic or ideological concerns were also at work where scholars sought to emphasize the alien character of the Essenes in the context of ancient Judaism, especially where this was accompanied by a positive evaluation of the sect. In such cases, rabbinic Judaism was viewed as repugnant or deficient, and the Essenes had to be redeemed by showing that they derived from a quite different ideology.

This is not to suggest that all scholarly positions were shaped by dogmatic prejudice. Many scholars simply tried to assimilate the Essenes to the material with which they themselves were most familiar—Greek philosophy in the case of Eduard Zeller, Hellenistic Judaism in the case of Moritz Friedländer, the apocalyptic literature for Hilgenfeld, or the rabbinic tradition for Zecharias Frankel. But ideological considerations indisputably played a significant part in the debate. None of these assessments of the Essenes was entirely without basis. Both Philo and Josephus noted the importance the Essenes attached to the study of scriptures, and also noted their great concern for purity. The latter concern provides a plausible explanation for the separation of the Essenes from the rest of Judaism. Yet the accounts of the Essenes by Philo and Josephus emphasize the dualism of body and spirit associated with the Pythagoreans, and the common life of the Essenes also brings to mind the ancient accounts of Pythagorean communities. The common life of the Essenes also inevitably brings to mind the early Christians as portrayed in the Book of Acts.

The Scrolls and the Essenes

When the Damascus Document was published in the early twentieth century, it was attributed to "an unknown Jewish sect" in the words of Louis Ginzberg.[10] To be sure, various known Jewish sects were proposed. The first editor, Solomon Schechter, dubbed it a "Zadokite" work and supposed that it derived from a group of Sadducean origin. Various scholars attributed it to Dositheans or Samaritans, or even to the much later Karaites. But no one attributed it to the Essenes. When the Scrolls were discovered, however, the attribution to the Essenes was almost instantaneous, even though these texts were quickly seen to be related to the document from the Geniza.

The attribution of the Scrolls to the Essenes was the result of two considerations, neither of which had applied to the Damascus Document. First was the location of discovery, in an area where Pliny had located an Essene community. Second was the similarity between the description of the Essenes by Josephus and that found in the Community Rule or Manual of Discipline. The most striking similarities concerned the process of admission and the common life, but they extended even to minor details. Some of these, to be sure, were commonplaces, that one might expect to find in any association: respect for elders, a prohibition of spitting in the assembly, provision for expulsion. Even the common meal was a standard feature of the life of many associations in antiquity. But other features were more distinctive. Chief among these was the holding of property in common. Such a practice was known from Greek descriptions of utopian groups, including the Pythagoreans, but was not attested in any Hebrew source until the discovery of the Community Rule. The process of admission outlined in the Rule also provided the closest known parallel to that of the Essenes. Each required an initial probationary period (specified as one year in the case of the Essenes), followed by two more years, and the stages were marked off in relation to degrees of purity. There are minor discrepancies between the Greek and Hebrew accounts, but most interpreters have been more impressed by the similarities.

The Essenes, like the sectarians of the Scrolls, had a problematic relationship to the Jerusalem temple. Philo says that "they have shown themselves especially devout in the service of God, not by offering sacrifices of animals, but by resolving to sanctify their minds" (*Quod Omnis* 75). Josephus says that they send offerings to the temple, but follow different rituals of purification and are barred from entering the common enclosure. He says that they offered sacrifices separately, on their own. The evidence of the Scrolls is ambiguous. The Damascus Document forbids members to enter the temple "to kindle his altar in vain" (CD 6:11) but leaves open the question whether they offered sacrifices on their own. The Community Rule seems to regard the community as a replacement for the temple cult. While neither position is entirely clear, both the Scrolls and the Greek sources (Philo and Josephus) attest to a strained relationship with the temple.

Another important issue concerns the question of celibacy. The Greek and Latin accounts emphasize the celibacy of the Essenes, even though Josephus acknowledged that one branch of the sect permitted marriage. The Damascus Document clearly allows for married life, but seems to imply that this was not the case for all members of the sect. Damascus Document 7:4–7 contrasts those who walk in perfect holiness, who are promised that they will live for a thousand generations, with those who marry and have children. The Community Rule (1QS) does not mention women or children at all, despite its great concern with issues of purity, and has consequently been understood as a rule for a celibate community. It does not, however, make any explicit demand for celibacy.

Eventually, the interpretation of the site of Qumran would loom large in debates about the identification of the sect as Essene. It is useful to remember, then, that this identification was well established before the site was excavated at all. Roland de Vaux, who excavated Qumran, admitted from the outset that the role of archaeology was secondary, and that the Essene hypothesis could not be established by archeology alone: "There is nothing in the evidence to contradict such an hypothesis, but this is the only assured conclusion that we can arrive at on the basis of this evidence, and the only one which we can justifiably demand of it. The solution to the question is to be sought from the study of the texts, and not from that of the archaeological remains."[11] Even if the site of Qumran should prove to be, say, a military establishment rather than the home of a religious community, the identification of the Community Rule as an Essene document could still stand. To be sure, one major reason for thinking of the Essenes at all would be removed if the location of the Scrolls turned out to be coincidental, and they were not related to the site. But nonetheless, the identification does not stand or fall on the archeological evidence. We shall turn to that evidence in the next chapter, but for the present we will focus on the literary evidence for the identification with the Essenes.

Dissident Views

The Essene identification won wide acceptance almost immediately. Prominent scholars who endorsed it included Millar Burrows, Yigael Yadin, Geza Vermes, J. T. Milik, Frank Moore Cross, and the excavator of the site of Qumran, Roland de Vaux. There were always some dissenters. As in the case of the Damascus Document, nearly every known Jewish sect was proposed at some time by someone or other—Pharisees, Sadducees, Hasidim, Zealots, Ebionites, Karaites, and even Christians. Chaim Rabin, a German-born Jewish émigré who taught at Oxford before moving to the Hebrew University, argued that the Qumran sect was "a diehard Pharisee group trying to uphold 'genuine' Pharisaism (as they understood it) against the more flexible ideology introduced by the Rabbis in authority."[12] G. R. Driver, the *eminence grise* of semitic studies at Oxford, and Cecil Roth, an Oxford-trained Jewish historian, thought they were the Zealots in the war against Rome, because of the militant ideology of the War Scroll.[13] The Sadducees were proposed early on, and again in the 1980s, when some of the halachic positions in a text known as 4QMMT ("Some of the works of the Torah") were found to agree with the Sadducees against the Pharisees. The idea that Scrolls were the documents of early Christianity was put forward by maverick scholars, Barbara Thiering[14] and Robert Eisenman.[15] While some of these suggestions are more fantastic than others, none of them has won the support of scholars. The durability of the Essene identification is due in no small part to the lack of a plausible alternative.

A Major Jewish Sect

The weightier objections to the Essene hypothesis have not been tied to alternative proposals, but are content to assign the Scrolls to "an unknown Jewish sect." In an article published in 1952, Saul Lieberman noted similarities between the Community Rule from Qumran and the regulations of the Haverim in rabbinic literature.[16] These were early Pharisees who formed associations for table fellowship with strict purity requirements. Like the Qumran sect, they had a process of gradual admission over a period of time. Lieberman warned that many sectarian groups may have had similar regulations, and asserted that Palestine "swarmed" with sects around the turn of the era. Frank Moore Cross allowed that this was the strongest argument raised against the Essene hypothesis, but he countered that this argument had plausibility only when a few manuscripts of uncertain date were known. By the mid-1950s it was apparent that the Qumran sect was not one of the small ephemeral groups of the first century CE. On the contrary, it lasted for some two hundred years and had amassed a huge library. It was not confined to the site of Qumran. We should expect, then, that it could be identified with one of the major sects mentioned by Josephus. In the early days of research on the Scrolls, there was a tendency to argue that the sect could be identified as Essene by a process of elimination: neither the Pharisees, the Sadducees, nor the Zealots separated themselves from the rest of Judaism to this degree. Few scholars now believe that Josephus' account of the Jewish sects can be taken as exhaustive. Nonetheless, the actual evidence for sects in Judea around the turn of the era is quite limited, and the Scrolls fit the Essenes better than any of the others. In a frequently quoted passage Cross concluded:

> The task, therefore, is to identify a major sect in Judaism. To suppose that a major group in Judaism in this period went unnoticed in our sources is simply incredible. The scholar who would "exercise caution" in identifying the sect

of Qumran with the Essenes places himself in an astonishing position: he must suggest seriously that two major parties formed communistic religious communities in the same district of the desert of the Dead Sea and lived together in effect for two centuries, holding similar bizarre views, performing similar or rather identical lustrations, ritual meals and ceremonies. He must suppose that one, carefully described by classical authors, disappeared without leaving building remains or even potsherds behind; the other, systematically ignored by the classical sources, left extensive ruins, and indeed a great library. I prefer to be reckless and flatly identify the men of Qumran with their perennial houseguests, the Essenes.[17]

Cross's argument rested in part on the assumption that the Scrolls were the library of a community that lived at the site, but even if one were to restrict the argument to the literary evidence, it retains considerable force.

It is not, however, absolutely conclusive. Some discrepancies remain troubling. Minor differences in the accounts of the admission process can be accounted for easily enough, since practice may have varied over time, although it may be argued that sectarian disputes often turn on minute differences.

It is surprising, however, that the requirement of celibacy is never explicit. Moreover, the emphasis on the celibacy of the Essenes had a distorting effect on the study of the Scrolls. Despite the testimony of Josephus that there was an order of Essenes who married, the great emphasis of the Greek and Latin sources has been on the celibacy of the sect. According to Pliny, the Essenes lived "without any woman." But even if a branch of the sect refrained from marriage, it is difficult to imagine that they lived entirely without interaction with women. At the very least they had mothers, probably sisters and other female relatives, and they could hardly avoid occasional contact with the opposite sex. Because of the assumption of celibacy, however, virtually no attention was paid to what the Scrolls have to say about women until the 1990s. Once the subject was raised, however, the Scrolls were found to have quite a lot to say about them. The Damascus Document allows for marriage. A wisdom text, which may not be strictly sectarian, speaks of mothers as an honorific category, parallel to fathers. In fact, the great emphasis of the Greek and Latin authors on celibacy is probably a distortion. Celibacy attracted attention precisely because it was exceptional. The fact that women play a part in the Scrolls is not in itself an argument against the Essene hypothesis, but it shows that any hypothesis is likely to function like blinders, obscuring some aspects of the material even as it illuminates others.

A second problematic issue concerns the apocalyptic beliefs of the sect. The Greek and Latin accounts of the Essenes give no hint of the apocalyptic and messianic ideas found in the Scrolls, even, indeed especially, those that are clearly sectarian. It was the presence of this material, as well as the fact that Qumran was evidently destroyed by the Romans during the Jewish revolt, that prompted scholars like Roth and Driver to attribute the Scrolls to the Zealots, and it has also contributed to Eisenman's eccentric view of early Christianity as a hate-filled revolutionary movement at odds with the account in the Gospels. Other scholars are troubled by the discrepancy between the eschatological militancy of some of the Scrolls and the depiction of the Essenes as a peace-loving community by Philo and Josephus.

Eschatological militancy is not necessarily incompatible with apparent pacifism in the present. According to the Community Rule (col. 10:16–21), the sectarian recognizes that "to God belongs the judgment," and consequently he should not be involved in any dispute with "the men of the pit" (the adversaries of the sect) *until the day of wrath*. To an outside observer, this might look like pacifism, but as often with apocalyptic groups, violence is only deferred to the proper time. It is not disavowed.

Nonetheless, scholars who identify the sect known from the Scrolls with the Essenes must contend that the Greek and Latin accounts are deficient. In fact, many scholars had doubted the reliability of these accounts long before the Scrolls were discovered. Jewish scholars, especially, beginning with Frankel in the nineteenth century, suspected that Philo and Josephus had exaggerated resemblances to movements, such as the Pythagoreans, known to Greek and Roman readers, and had omitted features that these readers might have found offensive. These suspicions were not without foundation. Josephus' comparison of the Essenes to the Dacians was not made for the benefit of Jewish readers. Moreover, Josephus scarcely acknowledges that any Jews held messianic or apocalyptic beliefs, so we should not be surprised that he does not report them in the case of the Essenes. There can be little doubt that he drew on Greek models in shaping his account. This does not necessarily discredit his information, but it calls for some caution in using it.

Nearly all scholars have agreed that the Essenes had deep roots in Jewish tradition, especially in their concern for purity and for the law of Moses, but that the preserved accounts also attribute to them distinctive features that have more in common with non-Jewish movements, such as Pythagoreanism. Scholarly disputes have centered on the relative weight to be placed on each of these aspects, and also on the degree to which the "Hellenizing" accounts of Philo and Josephus should be trusted. These debates could only be settled by the discovery of authentic Essene sources, authored by the sectarians themselves. Many scholars believe that precisely such documents were discovered in the Dead Sea Scrolls.

There is an awkward appearance of circularity in an argument that identifies the sect as Essene on the basis of the Greek and Latin accounts, and then proceeds to correct those accounts on the basis of the new evidence. Consequently, it is not surprising that doubts about the identification persist. Yet the similarities between the Qumran sect and the Essenes are striking, and no alternative proposal has been found plausible. In the writer's view, the Essene identification remains probable, but this is an issue on which reasonable people can disagree.

The ambiguity of the evidence, however, scarcely accounts for the passion with which the Essene hypothesis has been debated. At least in some cases (e.g., Norman Golb), scholars seem to feel that attribution to the Essenes impugns the authenticity of the Jewish character of the Scrolls, and diminishes their importance. (It should be noted, however, that there have always been staunch Jewish supporters of the hypothesis, beginning with Suke-nik and Yadin.) Conversely, for others the Essene hypothesis affirms the diversity of Second Temple Judaism and shows that a kind of Judaism that has often been considered marginal, and suspiciously akin to Christianity, was in fact a major presence in Judea around the turn of the era. These consider-ations are also at issue in the debates about the sig-nificance of the Scrolls for Judaism and Christian-ity, which we shall consider in later chapters.

Further Reading

The main ancient sources on the Essenes are help-fully presented, with translations, by Geza Vermes and Martin D. Goodman, *The Essenes according to the Classical Sources* (Sheffield: Sheffield Aca-demic Press, 1989). In addition to Philo, Josephus, and Pliny, they include passages from Dio of Pru-sa, Hegesippus, and Hippolytus. For a full discus-sion of the sources on the Essenes, see Joan E. Tay-lor, "The Classical Sources on the Essenes and the Scrolls," in Timothy H. Lim and John J. Collins, eds., *The Oxford Handbook of the Dead Sea Scrolls* (Oxford: Oxford University Press, 2010), 173–99.

For scholarship on the Essenes before the dis-covery of the Scrolls, see Siegfried Wagner, *Die Es-*

sener in der *Wissenschaftliche Diskussion vom Aus-
gang des 18. bis zum Beginn des 20. Jahrhunderts.
Eine Wissenschaftsgeschichtliche Studie* (BZAW 79;
Berlin: Töpelmann, 1960). A discussion of schol-
arship up to the middle of the nineteenth century
can be found in Christian D. Ginsburg, *The Essenes.
Their History and Doctrines* (London: Routledge &
Kegan Paul, 1955; originally published in 1864 by
Lund Humphries and Co.).

On the Essenes and the Pythagoreans, see Justin
Taylor, *Pythagoreans and Essenes. Structural Parallels* (Paris/Louvain: Peeters, 2004).

The parallels between Josephus's account of the
Essenes and the Dead Sea Scrolls are set out in detail by Todd S. Beall, *Josephus' Description of the Essenes Illustrated by the Dead Sea Scrolls* (Cambridge:
Cambridge University Press, 1988).

A forceful argument against the Essene hypothesis is made by Steve Mason, "Essenes and Lurk-
ing Spartans in Josephus' Judean War: From Story
to History," in Zuleika Rodgers, ed., *Making History: Josephus and Historical Method* (Leiden: Brill,
2007), 219–61.

For the author's assessment of the arguments, see
Collins, *Beyond the Qumran Community*, 122–65.

On women in the Scrolls, and the neglect of the
topic in modern scholarship, see Eileen Schuller,
"Women in the Dead Sea Scrolls," in P. W. Flint and

J. C. VanderKam, eds., *The Dead Sea Scrolls After Fifty Years: A Comprehensive Assessment* (Leiden: Brill, 1999), 2:117–44, and Sidnie White Crawford, "Not According to Rule: Women, the Dead Sea Scrolls and Qumran," in S. Paul, R. A. Kraft, L. Schiffman, and W. Fields, eds., *Emanuel: Studies in Hebrew Bible, Septuagint, and the Dead Sea Scrolls in Honor of Emanuel Tov* (Leiden: Brill, 2003), 111–50.

The Site of Qumran

The ruins of Qumran are located about nine miles south of Jericho, and thirteen miles east of Jerusalem, near the northern end of the Dead Sea. They stand on a marl plateau, with rocky cliffs to the west and a plain to the east. Wadi Qumran is to the south. They had been noted by travelers in the nineteenth century, as had the presence of burials nearby. One of the graves had been excavated. It was noted that the burials were not oriented east-west in the usual Muslim manner, but rather north-south. The rock-cut aqueduct and stepped pools had also been noted. The prevailing opinion was that there had been a small fortress at the site.

When the Scrolls were discovered, it was not immediately obvious that they were related to the site. De Vaux originally supposed that the ruins pertained to a Roman fort. When he and Lankaster Harding made soundings at Qumran at the end of 1951, they concluded that the quality of the buildings was too poor for a Roman fort. They found a jar embedded in the floor of one of the rooms that was of the same type as those in which scrolls had been found, and so they concluded that the Scrolls were related to the site after all. They also found similar pottery and oil lamps, and a coin dating to 10 BCE. They concluded that this was the site of the Essene settlement to the west of the Dead Sea of which Pliny had written. This in turn led to the inference that the Scrolls were the library of the Essene community that lived at the site.

De Vaux proceeded to excavate the site from 1953 to 1956. He had not published his findings in full at the time of his death in 1971, but he had published a comprehensive account of his interpretation of the site in his 1959 Schweich Lectures to the British Academy, which appeared in French in 1961 and in English with revisions in 1973.[1] A synthesis of his field notes was published in French by Jean-Baptiste Humbert and Alain Chambon in 1994, and in English by Stephen Pfann in 2003.[2]

The Phases of Occupation

The site of Qumran had apparently been occupied in the late Iron Age (8–7 century BCE). This was shown by a layer of ash with pottery shards from that period. From the presence of these shards, de Vaux reconstructed the plan of a rectangular building with a courtyard. This plan resembled other Judean fortresses, and so it was assumed that this had been a fortress too. De Vaux assigned a large round cistern to this period, although it did not contain Iron Age pottery. The fortress must have had a water supply, and this cistern differed from all the others insofar as it was round. This part of de Vaux's interpretation of the site has not been controversial. It is significant mainly in showing that the site was a suitable location for a military fort or lookout.

After the Babylonian exile, the site lay vacant for several centuries. It was reoccupied in the Hellenistic period. The Hellenistic settlement was characterized by a substantial tower on the northern side, some large rooms, apparently designed for assembly, and an elaborate water system. The main entrance was in the middle of the northern side, just north of the tower. A passageway divided the site into two parts. On the east was the main building, with the tower in the northwest corner. It consisted of rooms grouped around an open courtyard. The largest room, south of the main building, was identified as an assembly hall. Adjacent to it was a pantry, which contained more than a thousand dishes, suggesting that the large room also served as a dining hall or refectory. A channel collected rain water from the cliffs and delivered it to several cisterns and pools. Several of the pools had steps, and some had dividers, which strongly suggest that they were immersion pools for purification (*mikvaot*). (The dividers separated those going down from those coming up.) A few inkpots and fragments of tables appeared to have fallen from an upper story. De Vaux hypothesized that they came from a scriptorium, where the scrolls were copied. There was also evidence of pottery works. A large cemetery, with more than a thousand graves, was adjacent to the buildings. A long wall ran north-south for 150 yards, with the settlement to its west and the cemetery to its east. About one-third of this wall was attached to the buildings, while the remaining part was free standing. Half a mile south of Qumran, there was another building, by the spring of Ain Feshka. Another wall, found intermittently for 550 meters along the shore of the Dead Sea, connected Qumran to Ain Feshka.

De Vaux believed that very few of the rooms at Qumran were suitable for living quarters. Most would have been used for community purposes. Nonetheless, the number of graves nearby suggested a population of as many as two hundred people at any given time. There was, then, a manifest discrepancy between the number of graves and the number of people who could have been accommodated in the buildings. De Vaux inferred that while some of the leaders may have lived on the site, the majority of the residents must have lived outside the buildings. He distinguished between the natural caves in the cliffs and man-made caves in the marl terrace. Scraps of rope and mat and other artifacts were found in the latter, showing that they had in fact been inhabited. Some residents might also have lived in tents or huts. They would have been supported from the nearby farm at Ain Feshka. De Vaux's hypothesis that some people lived in caves was later confirmed by Israeli archeologists, Magen Broshi and Hanan Eshel, in the 1990s.[3] Some archeologists, however, remain skeptical. How would members who dwelled in caves make their way back to their quarters after late-night study sessions in the community center? Those who postulate that all members lived in the buildings, presumably on the upper floor, have to estimate a much smaller population, in some cases as few as ten to twenty people. In that case, however, it is difficult to explain the size of the cemetery.

The Hellenistic-Roman Site

De Vaux distinguished three periods in the Hellenistic-Roman settlement, with the first one subdivided in two:

Ia: A brief initial settlement. De Vaux dated this to the time of John Hyrcanus (135/4–104 BCE) or one of his predecessors.

Ib: The period when it got its definitive form. This period ended in destruction. The buildings of this period certainly existed in the time of Alexander Jannaeus (103–76 BCE), and, de Vaux suggested, may have been constructed under John Hyrcanus.

IIa: Reoccupation in the early Roman period, up to its destruction in 68 CE.

III: A brief period of Roman occupation.

This reconstructed history of the site was punctuated by destruction layers at the end of periods Ib and II. Apart from that, de Vaux relied on pottery typology, and on the coins found in the course of the excavation. He did not follow the kind of stratigraphic analysis that was being used by Kathleen Kenyon at Jericho at the time of the Qumran excavations, which carefully distinguished levels or strata, like layers of a cake. He used the same numbers for a single room or *locus* (the immediate area being excavated) from the beginning to the end of the excavation, instead of changing the number for different levels. Kenyon was a pioneer in this regard, at least in the area of Palestinian archeology. The stratigraphic method only became standard more than a decade or so later. When Yigael Yadin excavated Masada in the 1960s, he designated *loci* in the same way that de Vaux had done at Qumran, without distinguishing different strata. De Vaux was not exceptional in this regard, but his method was one that later became outdated.

Jodi Magness, who generally follows de Vaux's interpretation of the site, has questioned whether his period Ia actually existed. It is not supported by distinctive coins or pottery. Eleven coins of John Hyrcanus (135/4–104 BCE) were found, but coins typically remain in circulation for some time. The largest number of coins found at the site (143) date from the reign of Alexander Jannaeus. Consequently, Magness dispenses with de Vaux's period Ia and moves the date of occupation of the site down to 100 BCE, at the earliest, and allows that it could have been as late 50 BCE.[4]

One suspects that de Vaux was trying to reconcile the results of the archeology with the emerging consensus about the date of the sectarian movement in the Scrolls. The Damascus Document began with a schematic history of the sect: "And in the age of wrath, three hundred and ninety years after He had given them into the hand of King Nebuchadnezzar of Babylon, he visited them and caused a plant root to spring from Israel and Aaron to inherit his land . . . and they perceived their iniquity and recognized that they were guilty men, yet for twenty years they were like blind men groping for the way" (CD 1:3–11). Then God took pity on them and raised up for them a Teacher of Righteousness. If the exile is dated to 586 BCE, and these figures are taken literally, the sect would have begun in 196 BCE, and the Teacher would have come on the scene two decades later. Everyone recognized that the number 390 was taken from Ezekiel 4:5 and could not be pressed for precise calculation in this way. Nonetheless, it was taken as evidence that the sect had its beginnings in the second century BCE. It was then suggested that the "period of groping" corresponded to the period of the Hasidim, who were active in support of the Maccabees, and who had, incidentally, often been suggested as the matrix from which the Essenes emerged. Moreover, the *Pesher* or Commentary on the book of Habakkuk (one of the initial batch of scrolls discovered; see chapter 1) tells of a conflict between the Teacher and the "Wicked Priest," who was apparently a High Priest. This led to the further conjecture that the sect withdrew from society because of a dispute over the High Priesthood. In 152 BCE, Jonathan Maccabee, brother of Judas Maccabee who had been killed in battle, assumed the High Priesthood, although he was not from the traditional line of High Priests. The designation "sons of Zadok" which is used for the sectarians in the rule books was thought to refer to the High Priestly line, and to indicate that the Qumran sect was founded by priests ousted from Jerusalem. J. T. Milik proposed that Jonathan was the Wicked Priest. Frank Cross preferred Jonathan's brother Simon, who became High Priest ten years later. Cross's preference was due in part to discomfort with pushing back the date of the founding of Qumran too far before the time of John Hyrcanus, because of the evidence of the coins. Milik's theory prevailed, however, and the date 152 BCE has often been given for the founding of the settlement of Qumran as if this were assured fact. None of this was well founded, and it would all be challenged in time, but it was supported by a broad array of scholars and the consensus dominated the field for half a century.

De Vaux recognized that the identity of the Teacher or of the Wicked Priest could not be established on the basis of archeological evidence, but he argued: "archaeology does provide a chronological framework, and thereby prescribes certain limits for the possible hypotheses."[5] This is true in a general sense: the site was evidently occupied for much of the first century BCE, and the first century CE up to the time of the Jewish revolt. But the interpretation of the archeological evidence was also sometimes influenced by scholarly hypotheses based on the texts. This seems to have happened with de Vaux's Phase Ia, or at least with his dating of it, which tried to make the archeological record seem compatible with the prevailing hypothesis about sectarian origins.

The buildings on the site suffered destruction twice. The second destruction, at the hands of the Roman army, can be dated to 68 CE, in the course of the first Jewish revolt against Rome. The first one is somewhat more controversial. De Vaux found evidence of destruction by earthquake, but also by fire. Josephus (*Ant* 15.121–47; *JW* 1.370–80) reports a major earthquake in the seventh year of Herod the Great (31 BCE). De Vaux supposed that this was the earthquake in question, and also that the fire was caused by the earthquake, although the evidence was inconclusive. Other possibilities have been suggested. The site might have been burned by the Parthians who invaded the region in 40–39 BCE. There were other earthquakes, at much later times (363 CE; 749 CE). Since the damage from the earthquake was not repaired, it might be simpler to suppose that it occurred when the site was no longer inhabited.

In any case, the site lay vacant for some time in the first century BCE. The water system was disrupted, as can be seen from sediment above the layer of ash from the fire. Only ten coins from Herod's reign were found (plus one more later), so de Vaux concluded that the site was vacant for most of Herod's reign, for a period of about thirty years. A hoard of

561 silver pieces in three pots was found beneath Period II but above Period Ib. The latest coin in the hoard dates from 9/8 BCE. De Vaux suggested that the hoard was buried either while the site was vacant or when it was reoccupied. This reconstruction has been questioned by Jodi Magness, who reasons that it was more likely to have been buried when the site was being abandoned. She also questions how long it lay unoccupied. In her view, the site was probably destroyed shortly after 9/8 BCE, the date of the latest coin, possibly during the upheavals that followed the death of Herod the Great in 4 BCE.[6] On this reconstruction, the paucity of coins from the reign of Herod is surprising.

The time of the abandonment of the site is of potential significance, since some scholars have suggested that the site may have had a change of occupants in the course of the first century BCE.

The dates of abandonment and reoccupation of the site determine the beginning of de Vaux's period II. The destruction by the Romans in or about 68 CE is not in dispute.

Interpretations of the Site

De Vaux's interpretation of the site was guided by the assumption that it was the home of the sectarian community described in the Scrolls, especially the Community Rule (1QS). That community bore a striking resemblance to Christian monasteries of a later age. While de Vaux refrained from calling the site a monastery, he borrowed Latin terms from Christian monastic life to label some of the rooms—the large room near the pantry was a "refectory," and the upstairs room from which inkpots and tables had fallen was a "scriptorium." Many of the pools were understood to serve the purification rituals of the sect. One of the more puzzling discoveries consisted of animal bones that were deposited between large pottery shards, or sometimes placed in jars, in the spaces between and around the buildings. De Vaux suspected that these might have been the remnants of sacrificial meals, although he did not find anything that could be interpreted as an altar. In any case, he concluded that these deposits were clear evidence that some of the meals eaten in the main chamber had a religious significance. Other possible interpretations can, however, be imagined. The bones from ordinary meals might have been buried so as not to attract scavenging animals.

Most scholars have found this interpretation of the site persuasive. Frank Moore Cross wrote that "all these details dredged up by spade and trowel admirably illustrate the life of the community of which we read in classical texts dealing with the Essenes and in the scrolls themselves."[7] For the fiftieth anniversary of the discovery of the Scrolls in 1997, the Israel Museum mounted an exhibit on "A Day at Qumran," based entirely on the assumption that the site was an Essene settlement.[8] Jodi Magness, the most influential interpreter of the archaeology of Qumran since de Vaux, strongly affirms his interpretation of the site as a religious settlement.

Beginning in the 1980s, however, dissenting voices have been raised. In the following decade or so, several attempts were made to explain the site without reference to the Scrolls. Robert Donceel and Pauline Donceel-Voûte, Belgian archaeologists who had been invited to help prepare some of de Vaux's material for publication, suggested that Qumran was a *villa rustica*, or rural estate.[9] They were impressed by fragments of glass and other objects which they took to indicate a measure of luxury. Most scholars found the idea of a luxury villa on the shores of the Dead Sea in the arid Judean desert to be frankly ludicrous, but some other archeologists found merit in the idea. Yitzhar Hirschfeld, who held that the site was initially a fort, argued that it was later the center of a rural estate, a local version of the Roman villa rustica.[10] Like the Donceels, he was impressed by the presence of glass and some fine ware, admittedly in small quantity. In his view, the most striking feature of Herodian Qumran was the industrial installations, such as potter's workshop, winepress, and mill. He argued that the building, with its fortified tower, resembled other manor houses in Herodian Palestine.

Jean-Baptiste Humbert, de Vaux's successor at the École Biblique, thought the Qumran settlement "reminiscent of the Pompeiian *villa*," although he saw more resemblance to the urban *domus* than to the villa rustica.[11] (Humbert, nonetheless, believed that it was occupied by the Essenes in the first century CE.)

Other scholars, however, have been impressed with the poverty of the site. Magness finds the pottery to be plain and repetitive. Fine ware is either rare or not represented at all. Magness made a thorough comparison of Qumran with the manor houses adduced by Hirschfeld.[12] While some of these had towers similar to the one at Qumran, they also had various Roman features that are lacking in the site by the Dead Sea: Roman-style bath house with a heating system, mosaics, amphoras, etc. If Qumran was a villa, it was an exceptionally poor one. Moreover, some resemblance to a villa is not incompatible with a religious settlement, a point acknowledged by Humbert. Neither is the presence of some luxury items. Christian monasteries in the Middle Ages were often quite wealthy, although the monks took vows of poverty. A religious settlement might also be expected to have workshops, pottery kilns, etc. Even monks have to support themselves.

In 1994, two Australian scholars suggested that Qumran was a trading post or a station for caravan trade.[13] They believed that there was significant commercial traffic on the Dead Sea and a major trading route along its western shore. Most scholars think this view is at best exaggerated. The Dead Sea was higher in antiquity, and it is unlikely that there would have been room for a road below Ras Feshka, to the south of Qumran. We need not assume that Qumran was an isolated location. It was not far from Jericho, or even from Jerusalem. But it was hardly the site of a major crossroads.

Yizhak Magen and Yuval Peleg, prominent Israeli archeologists who conducted excavations at Qumran in the years 1996 to 2002, proposed that Qumran was primarily a pottery factory (although initially it had been a military fort).[14] The main purpose of the elaborate water system, with its stepped pools, was, supposedly, to provide potter's clay. The basis for this claim is that the largest reservoir was found to contain a thick layer of clay, which they describe as "high-quality potter's clay." Unfortunately they do not support this claim with any parallels that would illustrate what a pottery factory might be expected to look like. Neither do they provide any evidence that the pottery found at the site was made from clay collected from the pools. In fact, about half the vessels that have been analyzed appear to have been made from Jerusalem clay. Magness argues that it would be difficult to transport pottery from Qumran to other locations because of the problem of breakages. But in any case, the proposal that Qumran was designed for the manufacture of pottery can hardly be taken seriously without some supporting evidence. It would be difficult to explain the adjacent cemetery, let alone the scrolls in the adjacent caves, on this hypothesis.

Of the various alternatives that have been proposed to the interpretation of Qumran as a religious site, by far the most plausible is that it was a military fort. Everyone agrees that there was a fort on the site in the pre-exilic period. It was destroyed by force during the war against Rome. De Vaux believed that the Romans maintained a garrison there after the destruction of 68 CE. He noted the strategic value of the site, since it offers a view over the whole of the western shore of the Dead Sea from the mouth of the Jordan to Ras Feshka.[15] The ruins at Qumran are obviously not those of a fortress. Only the tower is fortified. But the site could have had military value as a lookout point.

Moreover, in the Hasmonean era there was a chain of fortresses in the area of the Dead Sea.

These were built in the reigns of John Hyrcanus (135–104 BCE), Aristobulus (104–103), and Alexander Jannaeus (103–76). They extended from Alexandrion-Sartaba and Dok, near Jericho, on the northern end, to Masada in the south. The fortress of Kypros guarded the main road to Jerusalem. There were fortified docks on the Dead Sea south of Qumran. Hyrcania was not far inland, and even Herodium, southeast of Bethlehem, was not very far away. Across the Dead Sea was Machaerus, built by Alexander Jannaeus to guard against the Nabateans. (See map of the Dead Sea Region.) It is difficult to believe that the Hasmonean kings would have allowed a site of even modest strategic value in the middle of the area ringed in by fortresses, to be occupied by a sectarian movement that is generally believed to have been hostile to them.[16] This problem would have disappeared after the Roman conquest of 63 BCE, which brought about the collapse of Hasmonean power.

The question arises, then, whether the site might have been a fortress in Hasmonean times, but converted to other use after the Roman conquest. Several archeologists have in fact suggested such a scenario (Hirschfeld, Magen, and Peleg, and most recently Robert Cargill).[17] Typically, these scholars point to a square structure in the middle of the complex, with the tower at its northwest corner.

They reason that this square structure was the original nucleus of the site, and that it was a fort. (It corresponds essentially to the old Iron Age fort.) The other buildings evolved outward from this. This reasoning assumes that the original buildings followed a coherent plan. We have noted already that de Vaux did not follow the stratigraphic method that subsequently became standard. Without clear stratigraphic evidence, arguments about the order in which buildings were constructed remain hypothetical, even if they have some *prima facie* appeal. It is worth noting, however, that de Vaux also supposed that when the site was reoccupied in the Hellenistic period, it began as a small structure along the lines of the old Iron Age fort, and was only expanded in a second phase (phase 1a).

It obviously makes a huge difference whether the Scrolls are thought to have come from the site. Most scholars remain persuaded that the proximity of the caves to the ruins was not mere coincidence. This is especially true in the case of Cave 4, and of the other caves in the marl terrace. The people who put the scrolls in these caves could scarcely have done so without going through the settlement. This does not necessarily require that all the scrolls belonged to the library of the community at Qumran, but it does require that there was a friendly relationship between the people who hid the Scrolls and those who dwelt at the site. Accordingly, most scholars accept that the site was a religious settlement in de Vaux's phase II, which is to say, in the first century CE down to the time of destruction.

Besides the proximity of the caves to the site, the main argument that it was a religious settlement arises from the number of stepped pools, which are most reasonably interpreted as *mikvaoth*, immersion pools for purification. Given the location in the desert, it is not surprising that the water system is a striking feature of the site. There are three large pools without steps. It is estimated that these pools would have preserved enough water for the inhabitants and their animals in the dry season. Ten other pools (out of a total of sixteen) have been identified as mikvaoth. Some of these have small partitions on the stairs to separate the pure from the impure. These pools are larger than contemporary mikvaoth, but this fact can be explained by the desert location and by the size of the community. They occupy approximately 17 percent of the site. In some private houses in Jerusalem, near the gates of the Temple Mount, mikvaoth occupy about 15 percent of the space, but these were presumably for the use of priests who were very numerous in the Temple area. A similar density in a desert location is quite another matter, and would be difficult to explain if the site was not inhabited by a religious community that was greatly concerned with purity. None of the manor houses in Judea in this period had a comparable density of mikvaoth.

It is clear that some of these mikvaoth were constructed before the earthquake, but even if this is identified with the earthquake of 31 BCE, this was more than thirty years after the Roman conquest. Whether they were part of the settlement before the coming of the Romans, we simply do not know. (In fact, Jodi Magness's dating of the occupation of the site, 100–50 BCE, allows for the possibility that it may not have been occupied at all before the Roman conquest.) The hypothesis that it was a fort in the Hasmonean period is just that—an hypothesis. But equally, the usual view that it was from the beginning a religious settlement is hypothetical. Here we suffer the consequences of the fact that de Vaux had not yet come to appreciate the stratigraphical method. If the site had been excavated twenty years later, the situation would presumably have been different. It should be noted however, that no one has found clear archeological evidence that the site was occupied by different groups in the first century BCE. There is no indication of a change in the kinds of pottery or other artifacts from one period to another.

The Cemetery

The cemetery adjacent to the ruins presents a whole set of problems on its own. De Vaux identified about 1,100 tombs. Later counts have varied slightly, but there are at least 1,050. There are actually three cemeteries: the main one just east of the ruins, one south of Wadi Qumran, and one to the north, about a ten-minute walk away. The largest part of the main cemetery lay to the west, quite close to the ruins. Four extensions spread eastward like fingers. De Vaux excavated forty-three graves in all—twenty-eight in the main cemetery, nine in the extensions, two in the northern cemetery, and four in the southern. Ten more graves were later excavated by Solomon Steckoll, in 1967. All of these were simple shaft tombs, covered by a pile of stones. Most were without grave goods, but a few had fragments of pottery, remains of wooden coffins, and jewelry. In contrast, most Judeans of the period were buried in family tombs. Some scholars have inferred that the cemetery at Qumran was especially well suited to a celibate sect. Individual shaft tombs, however, have been found at a number of other sites. Some of these are in the region of the Dead Sea, including a large Nabatean cemetery at Khirbet Qazone, to the southeast of the Sea, and En el-Ghuweir, south of Qumran. Some shaft tombs have also been found in

Jerusalem, and in a few other places. The cemetery at Khirbet Qazone shows that this style of burial was not the peculiar custom of a Jewish sect, and may have been a regional phenomenon. But the fact that a particular practice followed regional custom does not prove that it could not have been adopted by a Jewish sect.

Norman Golb argued that the cemetery was "obviously better interpreted as the graves of the warriors who fought at Qumran," and that the regular rows showed that all the graves were dug at once.[18] But this would have required a major battle at the site, of which we have no record. Moreover, the Jews would presumably have lost that battle, and then we would have to wonder who buried the dead in such an orderly manner after the defeat? There is no comparable cemetery adjacent to any other fort in Judea.

The most controversial aspect of the cemetery has been the presence of female skeletons. The excavations, including the later one by Steckoll, yielded fifty-eight skeletons. The initial studies identified eleven of these as female and six as infants. These figures were later revised slightly. (It is not so easy to distinguish female skeletons from male ones after two thousand years; the identification often depends on the size and proportion of the skeleton.) A revised estimate increased the number of female skeletons to thirteen or fourteen. The issue is complicated, however, by the possibility that some of these skeletons were not those of ancient Jewish women but of Bedouin, interred no more than two hundred years ago. Three graves with female skeletons contained jewelry. Some others were oriented east-west, whereas most of the graves in the cemetery were north-south. Moreover, several of the female burials were in the extensions of the cemetery rather than in the main part.

Everyone agrees that at least two or three of the skeletons excavated in the main cemetery were female. The sample of graves excavated is small, and the excavations of Jewish graves is an extremely contentious issue in modern Israel, because of the objections of orthodox Jews, so more extensive excavation is not a realistic option. It appears most likely that women were present at Qumran, but in disproportionately small numbers.

Pliny, in his account of an Essene settlement by the Dead Sea, claimed that the inhabitants lived "without women." Some scholars have assumed that the presence of any female skeletons disproves the Essene hypothesis. But this is hardly a reasonable position. The graveyards of Christian monasteries often contain female burials, even though the monks undoubtedly professed celibacy. The women may have been responsible for cooking and cleaning, or may have been relatives of the monks. We know from Josephus that some Essenes married. Here, as on many other issues, the evidence of archeology is inconclusive.

The cemetery is located about forty yards east of the site. This distance would satisfy minimally the rabbinic requirement for separating a dwelling from a burial site. It is possible that some graves were closer still. Some have been detected by ground-penetrating radar as close as ten meters to the site, but these have not been excavated. In light of the great emphasis on purity in the Dead Sea Scrolls, the proximity of the cemetery to the site is surprising. Various explanations have been offered, all speculative. Since the sectarians rejected the temple cult, they had no ritual means of remedying corpse impurity, and so there was no point to worrying about it. Or the sect may have believed that the sectarian dead were not defiling in the manner of other corpses. The cemetery was still separated from the buildings by a wall. Nonetheless, the proximity of the cemetery is an embarrassment for those who hold that Qumran was a religious, Essene, purity-obsessed settlement. Another embarrassment is caused by the discovery of a toilet in the middle of the settlement. The Temple Scroll required latrines to be 3,000 cubits outside the camp. This was farther than one was allowed to walk on the Sabbath, and coincidentally Josephus says that the Essenes did not relieve themselves at all on the Sabbath (*JW* 2.147). But while these apparent dangers to the purity of the settlement are problematic for the Essene hypothesis, they must be weighed in proportion to other considerations. The huge cemetery beside the settlement is even more problematic for theories that the site was a fort or a villa, since in those cases the number of burials is hard if not impossible to explain.

Was Qumran an Essene Settlement?

The hypothesis that the religious community described in the Community Rule was Essene was prompted in part by Pliny's mention of an Essene community to the west of the Dead Sea. That notice has also loomed large in the debate as to whether Qumran was an Essene settlement. Pliny is not very specific about the location of the Essenes. He says that they lived to the west of the Dead Sea, putting "the necessary distance between themselves and the insalubrious shore." Continuing his account, he says "below them (*infra hos*) is En-Gedi." Most scholars have taken this to mean that En-Gedi is to the south of the Essenes, since Pliny's account proceeds from north to south. Some, however, think that the point is relative elevation. Yitzhar Hirschfeld claimed to find evidence of a settlement of "hermits" on the cliffs above En-Gedi, but others have dismissed the ruins in question as the remnants of an agricultural installation, or shepherds' huts.[19] Pliny's account had never been taken to suggest the specific area of Qumran before the discovery of the Scrolls. It has even been suggested that he did not have any specific location in mind, but the location relative to En-Gedi makes this unlikely. The discovery of what seems to have been a community settlement at Qumran, equipped with numerous pools for purification, adjacent to the caves where the Scrolls were discovered, seems to most scholars to be too much for coincidence.

The identification of Qumran as an Essene settlement continues to command an overwhelming consensus. There are some problems, or at least surprising elements, such as the proximity of the cemetery, but all the alternative theories encounter greater ones. It is conceivable that the site was a fort in the Hasmonean period, in view of the prominence of multiple Hasmonean forts in the region. But even here, clear archeological evidence is lacking. It is also possible that the site was first inhabited by the Essenes, but after the demise of Hasmonean power. It is unfortunate that the site was not excavated with the stratigraphic methods that later became standard, and also that de Vaux did not live to publish his findings in full.

If we accept that the people who hid the Scrolls were either residents at Qumran or at least had some relationship to the inhabitants, the conclusion that the site was a sectarian settlement when the Scrolls were hidden is unavoidable. Scholars who resist this conclusion typically insist that the site should be interpreted without regard to the Scrolls. In view of the proximity of some of the caves to the site, however, especially in the case of Cave 4, such supposed scientific rigor is misguided. The Scrolls cannot be left out of account in the interpretation of the site. In fact, the Scrolls shed invaluable light on the interpretation of the site, by suggesting the kind of community that may have lived there. Conversely, the site sheds some light on the Scrolls, by providing a possible physical context for the community. One could, and indeed should, infer from the site that the inhabitants were greatly concerned with ritual washing, and so were presumably a religious community. The site alone, however, would hardly have ever led anyone to identify that community as Essene, or as the specific community described in the Community Rule. Without the texts, archeology is suggestive but seldom decisive.

The debate about the site of Qumran has often been heated, because of the assumption that the Essene hypothesis stands or falls with the interpretation of the site. This, however, is not so. The scrolls could conceivably describe an Essene community, or communities, even if Qumran was not occupied by one of them. The lively debate about the interpretation of the site, however, has not been fruitless. For a long time, Qumran was thought to be an isolated place in the wilderness, whose inhabitants were completely cut off from the outside world. Such an idea of complete isolation was unrealistic. It is now clear that the residents at Qumran had commercial relations of various sorts with other people in the region. The similarity of the pottery of Qumran to that of Jericho is a case in point. Even the burial customs may have been influenced by local custom in the Dead Sea region. Moreover, if the inhabitants were indeed the Essenes, we should expect that they were related to many other communities throughout Judah. Qumran was near Jericho, and not so far from Jerusalem. We do not have to imagine bustling activity on the Dead Sea to grant that the site was not as isolated as has sometimes been supposed. None of this, however, disproves the Essene hypothesis. It only calls for a more realistic assessment of how a religious community might have lived on the shore of the Dead Sea.

Further Reading

The classic account of the archeology of Qumran is still that of Roland de Vaux, *Archaeology and the Dead Sea Scrolls* (London: Oxford University Press, 1973). The most influential subsequent account is that of Jodi Magness, *The Archaeology of Qumran and the Dead Sea Scrolls* (Grand Rapids, MI: Eerdmans, 2002).

The most important alternative to de Vaux and Magness is the account of Yitzhar Hirschfeld, *Qumran in Context* (Peabody, MA: Hendrickson, 2004).

An important collection of essays, representing a spectrum of opinion, can be found in Katharina Galor, Jean-Baptiste Humbert, and Jürgen Zangenberg, eds., *Qumran: The Site of the Dead Sea Scrolls: Archaeological Interpretations and Debates. Proceedings of a Conference Held at Brown University, November 17–19, 2002* (STDJ 57; Leiden: Brill, 2006).

For recent assessments of the arguments, see Eric Meyers, "Khirbet Qumran and its Environs," in Timothy H. Lim and John J. Collins, eds., *The Oxford Handbook of the Dead Sea Scrolls* (Oxford: Oxford University Press, 2010), 21–45, and Collins, *Beyond the Qumran Community*, 166–208.

The Scrolls and Christianity

The Dead Sea Scrolls made available for the first time a corpus of literature in Hebrew and Aramaic from Judea around the turn of the era—from the time of Jesus of Nazareth. Much of the fascination that the Scrolls have held for the general public has arisen from the possibility that they might contain information pertinent to the career of Jesus that had been hidden, or perhaps suppressed, for nearly two thousand years. In the first decade or so after the discovery, scholarship on the Scrolls was preoccupied with their relevance to the New Testament. The exclusion of Jewish scholars from the official editorial team undoubtedly contributed to the imbalance of scholarship in this period, but it was inevitable that there would be great interest in whatever light these texts might shed on the origins of what would become the dominant religion of the Western world.

The stakes in the scholarly debate were construed in various ways. Scholarship on the New Testament had tended to view Christianity as a movement that took its decisive form when it moved beyond Judaism, into the Gentile, Hellenistic world. So, for example, it was thought that the belief that Jesus was the Son of God, or even God in some sense, could not have arisen in a Jewish context, but only in a pagan environment. Christian scholars often emphasized the novelty and even uniqueness of Christianity, and the boldness of its departure from Jewish precedents. The Scrolls provided an opportunity to test these assumptions against a substantial body of primary evidence from the Judaism of the time.

It was obvious from an early point that there were some significant analogies between the sectarian movement described in the Scrolls and the early church. Both were associations, with provision for admission and expulsion of members. Both practiced ritual washing in some form. Both had common meals and, at least in some cases, common possessions. Both had strong eschatological beliefs that the end of history was at hand, and expected the coming of a messiah or messiahs.

Some scholars tended to exaggerate these analogies. In extreme cases, a few scholars have even claimed that the Scrolls provide "nothing less than a picture of the movement from which Christianity sprang in Palestine," or rather "a picture of what Christianity actually *was* in Palestine."[1] Most were more moderate than that, but still there was endless fascination with the possibility that Jesus, or John the Baptist, might have known the Scrolls or the people they describe, and been influenced by them. Some pounced gleefully on similarities between the Scrolls and the New Testament, and inferred that Christianity was a derivative phenomenon, whose main insights were anticipated by another Jewish sect a century earlier. Others saw the points of continuity with the Scrolls as evidence that Christianity was indeed rooted in the Judaism of its day, and not a product of Hellenistic syncretism. It could therefore be viewed as an integral part of a tradition of divine revelation, going back to Mount Sinai, and as an authentic continuation of biblical tradition. In fact, it is difficult to say that the Scrolls have any bearing on the legitimacy or authenticity of Christianity, which depends on the acceptance of, or faith in, certain claims about Jesus (that he rose from the dead, and was Son of God in a unique sense) that cannot be either verified or falsified historically. Scholars have always known that Christianity began as a Jewish sect, and was influenced by Jewish traditions in manifold ways. But while the arguments about the authenticity and originality of Christianity may not have much rational force, they carry emotional power, and so the Scrolls have often been invested with theological importance that goes beyond logic and rationality.

Jesus and the Teacher, Phase One

The first scholar to argue for far-reaching analogies between the Scrolls and the New Testament was André Dupont-Sommer, a prominent French expert in semitic languages, who was also an early champion of the Essene hypothesis. In a communication to the *Académie des Inscriptions* in Paris on May 26, 1950, he invoked Renan's famous statement that Christianity was an Essenism that largely succeeded, and Essenism a foretaste of Christianity. He continued: "Today, thanks to the new texts, connections spring up from every side between the Jewish New Covenant, sealed in the blood of the Teacher of Righteousness in 63 BC and the Christian New Covenant, sealed in the blood of the Galilean Master around A. D. 30. Unforeseen lights are shed on the history of the Christian origins."[2]

Dupont-Sommer's view depended in large part on his interpretation of the *Pesher* or Commentary on the prophet Habakkuk, which was one of the first Dead Sea Scrolls to come to light in 1947. This

commentary interpreted the prophecies of Habakkuk with reference to events in Judean history in
the first century BCE, culminating in the Roman
conquest of Jerusalem under Pompey. It must have
been written around the middle of the first century BCE, or a little later. It also refers repeatedly
to a figure called "the Teacher of Righteousness,"
who also appears in the Damascus Document. The
righteous had been wandering like blind men until
God raised up the Teacher to guide them in the
way of his heart. In the *Pesher* on Habakkuk, the
Teacher appears as a prophetic figure, to whom the
true meaning of prophecy was revealed and whose
words were from the mouth of God. He was not
accepted, however, by the High Priest of the time,
who is called "the Wicked Priest" in the *Pesher*.

The confrontation between the Teacher and the
Wicked Priest is described in a controversial pas-
sage in column 11. The passage begins by quoting
Hab 2:15:

Woe to him who causes his neighbor to drink,
who pours out his fury (upon him) till he is
drunk, that they may gaze on their feasts!

The commentary follows:

The explanation of this concerns the Wicked
Priest who persecuted the Teacher of Righ-

teousness, swallowing him up in the anger of his fury in his place of exile. But at the time of the feast of rest of the Day of Atonement he appeared before them to swallow them up and to cause them to stumble on the Day of Fasting, their Sabbath of rest.

Dupont-Sommer insisted that the verb "to swallow" meant, in this instance, "to kill." He also argued that the Teacher then appeared, after his death, to swallow the Wicked Priest. In this way, he saw a parallel between the Teacher and Jesus, who had also been subjected to a violent death and who was expected to return to destroy the wicked.

"Everything in the Jewish New Covenant," wrote Dupont-Sommer, "heralds and prepares the way for the Christian New Covenant. The Galilean Master, as He is presented to us in the writings of the New Testament, appears in many respects as an astonishing reincarnation of the Teacher of Righteousness."[3] The Teacher, like Jesus, was the Messiah. He had been condemned and put to death, but he would return as the supreme judge. In the meantime, he too left a "church," supervised by an overseer or "bishop," and whose essential rite was the sacred meal.

Few scholars, either then or later, saw the similarities between Jesus and the Teacher as being as extensive as did Dupont-Sommer. The evidence that the

Teacher was condemned and put to death, or that he was expected to come again, is extremely dubious, to say the least. It is not clear that "swallowing" means "killing," and nearly all scholars agree that it was the Wicked Priest who "appeared" before the Teacher, disrupting his observance of the Day of Atonement. Dupont-Sommer defended, but also qualified, his views in several publications over the following decade. He insisted that he had never dreamt of denying the existence or the originality of Jesus. But the publicity surrounding his initial lecture and subsequent publications came at a price. Neither he nor any of his students was invited to join the international editorial team organized by Roland de Vaux, although he was eminently qualified. Moreover, his idiosyncratic reconstruction of the Teacher's death and supposed resurrection would reverberate through later scholarship for decades to come.

Dupont-Sommer also advanced another thesis that would continue to engage scholars more than half a century later. He held that both the Teacher and Jesus were modeled on the figure of the Suffering Servant, as found especially in the book of Isaiah, chapter 53. Of this figure it is said:

Surely he has borne our infirmities and carried our diseases . . .

He was wounded for our transgressions,
    crushed for our iniquities;
upon him was the punishment that made us
    whole,
and by his bruises we are healed. (Isaiah 53:4–5)

"Defining the mission of Jesus as prophet and savior," wrote Dupont-Sommer, "the primitive Christian Church explicitly applied these Songs of the Servant of the Lord to him; about a century earlier, the Teacher of Righteousness applied them to himself."[4] In this case, he could point to several passages in the Hodayot, or Thanksgiving Hymns, in which the speaker refers to himself as "thy servant." Many scholars have assumed that these hymns, or at least a cluster of them, were composed by the Teacher. In any case, even if the Hymns do model the Teacher on the Servant, it is not clear just what that entails. In Christian tradition, to say that Jesus is the Servant means not only that he suffered and was exalted but that he died for the sins of others. It is not at all clear that the "servant" in the Hodayot is thought to suffer vicariously in this way, or that he undergoes a sacrificial death. Nonetheless, the influence of the "Servant" passages in Isaiah remains a controversial issue.

Dupont-Sommer's views were taken up a few years later by the literary critic Edmund Wilson in a best-selling book, which originated in articles in the *New Yorker* magazine. Wilson was a perceptive observer, and one of the pleasures of his book lies in the sketches he provides of the leading characters. (He noted that de Vaux "does not in the least resemble any of the conventional conceptions of a typical French priest," and had "style, even dash.")[5] He recognized that the views of Dupont-Sommer were overstated. Nonetheless, he wrote, "if we look now at Jesus in the perspective supplied by the scrolls, we can trace a new continuity and, at last, get some sense of the drama that culminated in Christianity . . . The monastery [of Qumran] . . . is, perhaps, more than Bethlehem or Nazareth, the cradle of Christianity."[6] Wilson suggested that the scholars working on the Scrolls were "somewhat inhibited in dealing with such questions by their various religious commitments." He was not speaking only of the official editorial team, several of whom were Catholic priests. He suggested that there could be found among Jewish scholars "a resistance to admitting that the religion of Jesus could have grown in an organic way . . . out of one branch of Judaism," while among Christians there was fear "that the uniqueness of Christ is at stake."[7]

The fire of this controversy was fanned by three short radio broadcasts on the BBC Northern Home Service, in January 1956, by John Marco Allegro, a member of the editorial team. Allegro claimed that "recent study of my fragments has convinced me that Dupont-Sommer was more right than he knew."[8] Allegro pointed to another biblical commentary from Qumran, on the prophet Nahum, which was assigned to his lot. The commentary, or *pesher*, refers to a "lion of wrath" who "hangs men alive." This is usually taken as a reference to the Jewish king Alexander Jannaeus, who crucified hundreds of his enemies in the early first century BCE (Josephus, *Ant* 13.380; *Jewish War* 1.97). Allegro identified Jannaeus as the Wicked Priest, the adversary of the Teacher of Righteousness. He then inferred that the Teacher was one of the people crucified. "Most remarkable of all," he said, "is the manner of his death, and the significance attributed by his disciples to its consequences." He continued:

Probably hardly a decade after they had established themselves in their simple buildings at Qumran, the terrible Jannaeus, the Wicked Priest as they called him, stormed down to their new home, dragged forth the Teacher, and as now seems probable, gave him into the hands of his Gentile troops to be crucified. Already in Jerusalem this Jewish tyrant had displayed his bestiality by inflicting the same awful death on eight hundred rebels, and a Qumran Manuscript speaks in shocked tones of the enormity of this crime. For to a Jew, this death was the most accursed of all, since the body normally found no resting place but was left to moulder on the cross.

But when the Jewish king had left, (the sectarians) took down the broken body of their Master to stand guard over it until Judgment Day . . . In that glorious day, they believed their Master would rise again and lead his faithful flock (the people of the new testament, as they called themselves) to a new and purified Jerusalem.[9]

This broadcast caused an uproar. The *New York Times* published his views on February 5, 1956, under the heading "Christian Bases Seen in Scrolls." *Time* magazine followed on February 6 with an article entitled "Crucifixion before Christ." Allegro's colleagues on the editorial team were moved to respond. On March 16, 1956, a letter appeared in the *Times* of London signed by de Vaux, Milik, Skehan, Starcky, and Strugnell (all but the latter of whom were Catholic priests). They wrote:

We are unable to see in the texts the "findings" of Mr. Allegro. We find no crucifixion of the "teacher," no deposition from the cross, and no "broken body of their Master" to be stood guard over until Judgment Day. Therefore there is no "well-defined Essenic pattern into which Jesus of Nazareth fits," as Mr. Allegro is alleged in one report to have said. It is our conviction that either he has misread the texts or he has built up a chain of conjectures which the materials do not support.[10]

Frank Moore Cross's name did not appear in the list of signatories, but he wrote privately to Allegro:

Unless you have new data, which I have not seen in the pNah [pesher or commentary on Nahum], and which I am told via Jerusalem is not in the infamous Copper Document, you will have one hell of a time convincing me. If you have new data, I'll convince in a minute.[11]

Allegro did not have new data, and most scholars found his interpretation of *Pesher* Nahum unconvincing. He seems to have convinced himself, however, that he was being victimized by a conspiracy of Catholic clerics, intent on hiding the truth, despite the fact that Cross and Strugnell were Presbyterians. The controversy subsided. Allegro went on to commit definitive academic suicide by publishing a "grand, unifying theory of religion" called *The Sacred Mushroom and the Cross: A Study of the Nature and Origins of Christianity within the Fertil-*

ity Cults of the Ancient Near East (London: Hodder and Stoughton, 1970). He argued that Christianity was a variant of a kind of fertility cult common in the ancient Near East, involving sacred mushrooms, but that all explicit reference to these had been deceitfully suppressed. The word Boanerges, for example, the name given by Jesus to James and John, the sons of Zebedee in Mark 3:17, was supposedly the name of a sacred fungus. Even Allegro's most persistent (and unscholarly) defenders, such as the sensationalist British authors Michael Baigent and Richard Leigh, and Allegro's daughter Judith Anne Brown, could not accept this theory. For any educated student of religion it was simply ludicrous. As his daughter put it simply: "*The Sacred Mushroom and the Cross* ruined John's career."[12]

The Son of God

In a letter to de Vaux dated September 16, 1956, at the height of the controversy, Allegro wrote:

As for Jesus as a "son of God" and "Messiah" – I don't dispute it for a moment; we now know from Qumran that their own Davidic Messiah was reckoned a "son of God", "begotten" of God – but that doesn't prove the Church's fantastic claim for Jesus that he was God Himself. There's no "contrast" in their terminology at all – the contrast is in its interpretation.[13]

He was referring here to two texts, the Rule of the Congregation (1QSa), and the "Son of God" text (4Q246).

1QSa is an appendix to 1QS, the Community Rule or Manual of Discipline. It had not yet been identified when the "Manual" was first published in 1951, but it was published by Dominique Barthélemy in the first volume of the *Discoveries in the Judaean Desert* series in 1955.[14] It is a rule for the end of days. In the second column, lines 11–12, it prescribes the order for a banquet "when God begets the messiah with them." The reading of the word "begets" (*yolid*) is very difficult; the published photo is practically illegible at this point. The editor noted that after careful study with a transparency, the reading seemed practically certain, but in view of the awkward preposition "with them" he accepted a suggestion of Milik that the word was a scribal error, for *yolik*, brought or caused to go. Other readings would later be suggested. The scholars who examined the text in the 1950s, however, agreed that it read "will beget," whether this was a mistake or not. This reading has also been affirmed more recently on the basis of computer enhancement. The idea that God would beget the messiah has a clear basis in Psalm 2:7 and Psalm 110:3 (LXX) and so it is not especially surprising. While the reading is admittedly difficult, there are some grounds for suspecting that scholars, Jewish and Christian alike, were eager to emend it for theological reasons, because it seemed too similar to Christian ideas.

The second text to which Allegro alluded had not yet been published in 1956, although it had evidently been noted. This is an Aramaic text, 4Q246, officially called "Aramaic Apocalypse," but better known as "the Son of God" text. This was not made known to a wider public until December 1972, when J. T. Milik presented a lecture on the topic at Harvard University. It aroused great interest because some of its language is closely paralleled in the Gospel of Luke.

The text consists of two columns. The first is torn down the middle, so that only the second half of the lines survives. Someone is said to fall before a throne, and there is mention of a vision. The fragmentary text continues:

> affliction will come on earth . . . and great carnage in the provinces . . . the king of Assyria and [E]gypt . . . shall be great on earth . . . and all will serve . . . he shall be called, and by his name he shall be named.

The second column continues:

> Son of God he shall be called, and they will name him "Son of the Most High." Like shooting stars which you saw, so will their kingdom be. For years they will rule on earth, and they will trample all. People will trample on people and city on city until the people of God arises and all rest from the sword. His (or its) kingdom is an everlasting kingdom, and all his ways truth. He will judge the earth with truth, and all will make peace. The sword will cease from the earth, and all cities will pay him homage. The great God will be his strength. He will make war on his behalf, give nations into his hand and cast them all down before him. His sovereignty is everlasting sovereignty, and all the depths . . .

This text immediately brings to mind the story of the Annunciation in the Gospel of Luke. There the angel Gabriel tells Mary:

> And now you will conceive in your womb and bear a son, and you will name him Jesus. He will be great, and will be called the Son of the Most High, and the Lord God will give to him the throne of his ancestor David. He will reign over the house of Jacob forever, and of his kingdom

there will be no end. Mary said to the angel, "How can this be, since I am a virgin?" The angel said to her, "The Holy Spirit will come upon you, and the power of the Most High will overshadow you; therefore the child to be born will be holy; he will be called Son of God.

While the Gospel is in Greek and the new text is in Aramaic, the correspondence of several phrases is striking: "will be great," "Son of the Most High," "Son of God." Both texts speak of everlasting dominion.

Allegro evidently assumed that the Aramaic text referred to the Davidic messiah, a position that Frank Moore Cross is also known to have shared from an early point. Milik, however, argued that the figure who is called Son of God was not a Jewish messiah, but rather a Syrian king, probably Alexander Balas, a second-century BCE ruler who referred to himself on his coins as *theopator*, divinely begotten. The idea that the king was a negative figure relied on the assumption that a blank space before "until the people of God arises" marked a transition point in the text. Since the "Son of God" appears before this transition point, the argument goes, he is grouped with the enemies of God. In fact, apocalyptic texts seldom proceed in a simple unilinear manner, and so this argument is dubious. In any case, it must be weighed against the clear messianic usage of the titles Son of God and Son of the Most High in the Gospels. Milik's interpretation was not well received by the Harvard audience. Perhaps for this reason, he never published the text. Part of the text was published on the basis of Milik's handout, by Joseph Fitzmyer S. J., in 1974.[15] (Fitzmyer, a Jesuit priest, was evidently not suppressing the text for doctrinal reasons!) The official publication, by Émile Puech, did not follow until 1992.[16] Only at that point was it picked up by the popular media. Newspapers from London to Los Angeles trumpeted: "Son of God among the Dead Sea Scrolls!" suggesting that this had grave implications for Christianity.

The interpretation of this text has remained controversial. While Milik may not have won a following at Harvard, he has not lacked supporters, although some of them favor a different king (Antiochus Epiphanes, or even the Roman emperor Augustus, who was proclaimed *divi filius*, Son of God). Scholarship has been fairly evenly divided between those who favor the messianic interpretation and those who see this Son of God as a negative figure, even as an Antichrist. I would not want to suggest that resistance to recognizing this figure as the messiah is entirely due to theological considerations, but they have not been entirely absent.

For example, Fitzmyer takes the text to be speaking positively of a coming Jewish ruler, possibly an heir to the Davidic throne, but he insists that he is not a messiah, even though he admits that a successor to the Davidic throne in an eschatological context is by definition a messiah.[17] Some light may be shed on this paradoxical position by Fitzmyer's commentary on the parallel passage in Luke. He insists that the title "Son of God" is not used of a person who is called "messiah" in the Qumran text, and therefore does not have "a messianic nuance." He then goes on to insist that in the Gospel, "Son of God" attributes to Jesus a unique relationship with Yahweh, the God of Israel.[18] In this case, at least, the uniqueness of Jesus appears to be the issue at stake.

A Dying Messiah?

When the hitherto unpublished Dead Sea Scrolls became generally available in the early 1990s, a number of other texts attracted attention. One fragmentary text related to the war in the end-time was taken to predict the death of the messiah: "and they will kill the prince of the congregation, the Branch of David." The idea that the messiah would be put to death in the final war is attested in later Judaism, probably because of the fact that the messianic leader known as Bar Kochba was killed in the war against Rome of 132–135 CE. In the New Testament, however, it is clear that the death of Jesus came as a great shock to his followers, not as something that had been predicted. On inspection, however, this interpretation of the fragment proved to be improbable. The word translated as "they will kill" (*hmytw*) can also be rendered as " he will kill him," taking the Branch of David as the subject. Since the other messianic texts from Qumran uniformly present the Davidic or royal messiah as a mighty warrior who defeats the enemy, this interpretation is to be preferred.

A Prophetic Messiah?

A better parallel to the New Testament, however, is provided by a larger Hebrew fragment designated 4Q521 and sometimes dubbed "the messianic apocalypse," which begins: "heaven and earth will obey his messiah." The passage goes on to say:

> The glorious things that have not taken place
> the Lord will do as he s[aid] for he will heal the
> wounded, give life to the dead and preach good
> news to the poor.

This text brings to mind a passage in the Gospel of Matthew 11:

When John heard in prison what the Messiah was doing, he sent word by his disciples and said to him, "Are you the one who is to come, or are we to wait for another?" Jesus answered them, "Go and tell John what you hear and see: the blind receive their sight, the lame walk, the lepers are cleansed, the deaf hear, the dead are raised, and the poor have good news brought to them.

Both the Qumran text and the Gospel draw on Isaiah 61:1, where the prophet says:

The spirit of the Lord God is upon me, because the Lord has anointed me; he has sent me to bring good news to the oppressed, to bind up the brokenhearted, to proclaim liberty to the captives and release to the prisoners.

(This text is famously read by Jesus in the Capernaum synagogue, in Luke 4:18.) The Isaianic text does not mention raising the dead, and this suggests that the Gospel and the Qumran text had at least a further tradition in common.

In the Qumran text, it is God who is said to heal the wounded, give life to the dead, and preach good news to the poor. It is very odd, however, to have God preaching the good news: that was the work of a prophet or herald. Moreover, neither Isaiah 61 nor Matthew 11 has God as the subject. In Isaiah, the agent is an anointed prophet. The suspicion arises, then, that God is also thought to act through an agent in 4Q521, specifically, the "messiah" or anointed one whom heaven and earth obey. This messiah, however, is not a warrior king, but rather a prophetic "messiah" whose actions resemble those of Elijah and Elisha, both of whom were said to have raised dead people to life. If this is correct, then this Qumran text throws some genuine light on the career of Jesus, who certainly resembled Elijah more than a warrior king.

The expectation of a prophetic messiah appears only as a minor tradition in the Dead Sea Scrolls. 1QS 9:11 refers to "the coming of the prophet and the messiahs of Aaron and Israel," but most of the messianic references in the Scrolls concern the Branch of David, the messianic king. (4Q521 does not appear to be a sectarian text, but may have been part of the wider Jewish literature preserved in the Scrolls.) Jesus, however, does not seem well qualified for the role of warrior king in his earthly career. The possibility that he may first have come to be regarded as a messiah in the role of messianic prophet is intriguing. There are in fact indications in the Gospels that some people, at least, associated Jesus with Elijah. In Mark 6:14–15 various people identify Jesus to Herod as John raised from the dead,

Elijah, or "a prophet." Again in Mark 8:28, when Jesus asks "who do people say that I am?" he is told: "John the Baptist, and others, Elijah, and still others, one of the prophets."

Jesus and the Teacher, Phase Two?

The idea that the Teacher of Righteousness had applied to himself the passages about the suffering servant of the Lord in the Book of Isaiah, and thereby anticipated Jesus, was put forward in the early days of Scrolls research by Dupont-Sommer. It was revived in 1999 by Michael Wise, in a book entitled *The First Messiah. Investigating the Savior Before Christ* (San Francisco: Harper). In this case, the argument did not depend on newly published texts, but on the *Hodayot*, or Thanksgiving Hymns, which were among the first batch of Scrolls acquired by Sukenik in 1948. In the time between the work of Dupont-Sommer and that of Wise, the study of these hymns had been refined, by a distinction between Hymns of the Teacher and Hymns of the Community. In the Hymns of the Teacher, the speaker claims to be a mediator of revelation for others. He speaks of betrayal and rejection, and of his confidence that he will be vindicated. At least eight hymns of this type are clustered together in columns 10–17 of the *Hodayot* Scroll. (There is some disagreement about the precise delineation of the corpus.) These hymns have often been taken as the work of the Teacher of Righteousness, on the grounds that the sect can hardly have had more than one powerful personality of this type. Some scholars hesitate to accept this inference, and say that the hymns are formulaic, and could be applied to any member of the community. There is no doubt, however, that the speaking voice in these hymns is distinct from the rest of the *Hodayot*. It may never be possible to prove the authorship of these hymns without doubt, but "Teacher" here may serve as a designation for the speaker, whoever he actually was.

Wise claims that toward the end of the Teacher Hymns the Teacher came to speak of himself as the servant of the Lord in concentrated fashion, by alluding to the "servant" passages in Isaiah. He describes himself as stricken with afflictions, and forsaken, and repeatedly complains that people do not "esteem" him, using a Hebrew verb that is also used in Isaiah 53:3. He also claims to be endowed with the spirit. This claim recalls Isaiah 61: "The spirit of the Lord God is upon me, because the Lord has anointed me. He has sent me to bring good news to the oppressed." We have seen allusions to that passage also in 4Q521, which we discussed earlier.

The allusion to Isaiah 61 raises the question whether the Teacher may have been considered a messiah, perhaps the "prophetic messiah" envisioned in 4Q521. He was the one to whom God had made known all the mysteries revealed to the prophets, which the prophets themselves did not understand (*Pesher on Habakkuk*, col. 7). The coming of the Teacher was clearly thought to be an eschatological event, in the sense that he was ushering in the last phase of history. Neither in the hymns nor in the commentaries, however, is he ever called a messiah. Some scholars have pointed to a passage in the great Isaiah Scroll from Qumran Cave 1 (1QIsaᵃ), to argue that the "servant" of Isaiah 53 was understood as a messianic figure at Qumran. In Isaiah 52:4, where the traditional (Masoretic) text reads, "so his appearance was destroyed (*moshchath*) beyond that of a man," the Isaiah Scroll reads, "so I have anointed (*mashachti*) his appearance." The difference only involves the addition of one Hebrew letter at the end of the disputed word. It must be admitted that the traditional text makes much better sense in the context, and most scholars think the reading of the Qumran text is a simple scribal mistake. It opens up the possibility, however, that someone who read the Isaiah scroll from Qumran might well have inferred that the servant was anointed, and so a messiah. But nonetheless, the fact remains that the Teacher is never called a messiah explicitly.

Even if the Teacher was understood in terms of the suffering servant, however, and even understood as a messiah, how far could he be said to have anticipated Jesus? The Teacher was understood to have undergone suffering in the course of his mission. That mission was for the benefit of others. While the servant, in Isaiah 53:11, was said to make many righteous, the Teacher claims, "through me you have enlightened the face of the many" (1QHᵃ 12:27). But the Teacher is not said to offer his life as a ransom for many, or to suffer vicariously on their behalf. In contrast, in the New Testament we are told that "the Son of Man came not to be served but to serve, and to give his life as a ransom for many" (Mark 10:45), and in the epistle to the Romans 4:25 we are told that Jesus "was handed over to death for our trespasses and was raised for our justification." The servant of Isaiah 53 was usually understood in Judaism around the turn of the era as a paradigmatic case of humiliation followed by exaltation. (There is no clear allusion before the New Testament to the idea that his death would atone for others.) Both the Teacher and Jesus were afflicted and humiliated, and would be exalted. But the most novel aspect of the use of Isaiah 53 in the New Testament, which focused on the death of the servant as atonement for the sins of others, is not anticipated in the Dead Sea Scrolls.

The suffering servant appears again in a book by the Israeli scholar Israel Knohl, *The Messiah before Jesus. The Suffering Servant of the Dead Sea Scrolls* (Berkeley: University of California Press, 2000). Knohl's thesis is more far-reaching than that of Wise, and is based on a different text. This is the so-called Self-Exaltation Hymn, a fragmentary composition that survives in several copies, one of which is in a manuscript of the *Hodayot*. The speaker in this text also suffers contempt and rejection, but the emphasis is on his exaltation. The speaker boasts: "I am reckoned with the gods, and my dwelling is in the holy congregation," and that "there is no teaching comparable [to my teaching]." He speaks of a mighty throne in the council of the gods, and says that he has taken his seat in heaven. He boasts that his glory is with the sons of the king (= God), that he is a companion of the holy ones, and he even asks "who is like me among the gods?"

There is no agreement among scholars as to who the speaker in this text might be. Suggestions range from the Teacher of Righteousness to the eschatological High Priest. None of the Teacher Hymns makes such exalted claims for the speaker. In contrast, they have an acute sense of human unworthiness that is lacking in this composition. Another suggestion, that this hymn was put on the lips of the Teacher after his death, might allay this problem somewhat. The suggestion that the speaker is an eschatological figure is also hypothetical. We have no parallel for such claims by a messianic figure.

In Knohl's view, the speaker was a leader of the Qumran sect who saw himself as the messiah, and was recognized as such by his followers. Specifically, he identifies the sectarian leader as Menahem the Essene, who is said to have ingratiated himself to Herod by predicting that he would become king when he was still a boy. (Josephus, *Jewish Antiquities* 15.372–79.) While Knohl recognizes that "friend of the king" means "friend of God" in the hymn, he thinks that the choice of this language suggests that the speaker was also a friend of the human king of the day. He infers that he is the messiah, because in Psalm 110 the king messiah is invited to sit at the right hand of God. The references to suffering suggest that he is also the suffering servant. Since the Damascus Document says that the messiah of Aaron and Israel will atone for the sins of Israel, Knohl infers that the speaker in this hymn believed that his sufferings had atoning power. It is already obvious that this argument involves several intuitive leaps that are not required by the fragmentary evidence. Whether the figure in question is either messiah or servant is not beyond dispute. For

Knohl, however, this text is evidence that the association of the messiah with the suffering servant was not an innovation of early Christianity, but had already been made by this Jewish "messiah" a generation or so before the time of Jesus.

Knohl, however, goes further. In the Book of Revelation, chapter 11, John of Patmos has a vision in which two "witnesses" prophesy. They are identified as the two olive trees mentioned in a prophecy of Zechariah (chapter 4), and can therefore arguably be called "messiahs" (evidently, prophetic messiahs rather than royal ones). In the vision, they are killed by a beast that comes up from the bottomless pit. Their bodies lie in the street for three and a half days. Then the breath of life enters into them, they come back to life and are taken up to heaven. The Book of Revelation is a Christian composition, written toward the end of the first century CE. The death and resurrection of the witnesses is usually thought to be modeled on that of Jesus. Knohl argues, however, that it reflects an historical incident in 4 BCE, when Roman soldiers suppressed a revolt after the death of King Herod. (At the beginning of the vision, John is told to measure the temple but not the outside court, "for it is given over to the nations." The Roman soldiers in 4 BCE penetrated the courtyard of the temple but not the temple itself.) Since the copies of the "self-exaltation hymn" all date from the time of Herod, Knohl infers: "One can therefore assume that one of the two Messiahs killed in 4 BCE was the hero of the messianic hymns from Qumran."[19] So, he concludes, not only was the idea of a messianic suffering servant current before Jesus, but so was the belief that a messiah was raised after three days and exalted to heaven.

All of this argument involves huge intuitive leaps that go far beyond the available evidence. Knohl subsequently claimed to find confirmation of his theory in another controversial text, *The Vision of Gabriel*. This is a Hebrew text of some eighty-seven lines, written in ink on a slab of grey limestone. How exactly it was found is unknown, but it is alleged to come from the area east of the Dead Sea, and to have been discovered about the year 2000. It has sometimes been called "a Dead Sea Scroll on stone," but it is not part of the corpus of manuscripts found near Qumran. Its authenticity has not been challenged, although some doubts are inevitable in view of the uncertainty of its provenance. On the basis of the writing and the Hebrew it is thought to date from around the turn of the era.

The fragmentary text seems to be a speech of the angel Gabriel, promising imminent deliverance. It refers to David, at least twice. As Knohl reads it, it also refers to Ephraim, whom he takes to be another messianic figure known from later Jewish tradition. Other scholars read a different word instead of Ephraim. Crucial to Knohl's interpretation is another line, which he reads as "after three days, live." He infers that the messiah Ephraim would die and be raised after three days. The spelling of the word "live" is admittedly unusual: חיאה (the word "live" does not normally have an aleph in the middle). Other scholars suggest that the word should be read as האות, "the sign" (a word that occurs elsewhere in the text). So it is, to say the least, very uncertain that this text refers to resurrection, or indeed to a messiah Ephraim. Here again Knohl makes imaginative leaps to reach provocative conclusions, but very few scholars find his work persuasive.

What is at stake in this debate? It is, of course, entirely possible in principle that central affirmations of Christianity were derived from earlier Jewish ideas. The idea of a messiah is unequivocally Jewish. So is the idea that the messiah can be called "Son of God," despite the evident discomfort of some scholars on this point. The poems of the suffering servant in Isaiah were known, and used in various ways to express the experience of the suffering righteous, before the time of Jesus. Even the idea of resurrection after three days may have been prompted by a passage in the prophet Hosea, where certain Israelites in a time of distress express the hope that "after two days he will revive us; on the third day he will raise us up that we may live before him" (Hosea 6:2). But the evidence that a messianic figure before Jesus was construed as the suffering servant, and believed to have been raised from the dead after three days, is flimsy at best. Yet the attempt to find an exact prototype for Jesus in the Dead Sea Scrolls has fascinated people repeatedly for more than sixty years. The fascination of this mirage is obviously theological or ideological, but its implications are not at all clear: if Knohl were right, would this undermine the credibility of Christianity? or enhance it by showing that such ideas were grounded in Judaism? would it redound to the glory of Judaism, by showing the Jewish origin of influential ideas? or would it tarnish that glory by showing that some of the more "mythological" aspects of Christianity were at home in Judaism too? Or should it have any bearing on our judgments about Judaism or Christianity at all? What is clear is that the desire to prove, or disprove, claims that are thought to be fraught with theological significance can only distort the work of the historian.

John the Baptist

Not all debates about the Scrolls and early Christianity concern Jesus. The question whether John the

Baptist was a member of "the Qumran community" has proven to be a hardy perennial in this regard. The area where John had performed his baptisms was within walking distance of Qumran. The Essenes too had attached great importance to ritual washing. Even Joseph Fitzmyer, a scholar noted for his hard-headed sobriety and stern critiques of sensationalism, has held that the idea that John was a member of the Qumran community is "a plausible hypothesis," granted that "one can neither prove nor disprove it."[20] Fitzmyer even speculates that after the death of his elderly parents, John may have been adopted by the Essenes. Further, he claims that John's baptism may be seen as a development of the ritual washings of the Essenes, although it has a different character in the Gospels. More recently, the association of the Baptist with the sect has been argued by James Charlesworth. Charlesworth grants that the Baptist cannot have been a member of the Essenes in the phase of his career described in the New Testament, but supposes that he had gone through much of the initiation process and then withdrawn. This thesis, claims Charlesworth, "helps us comprehend the Baptizer's choice and interpretation of Scripture, especially Isaiah 40:3, his location in the wilderness not far from Qumran, his apocalyptic eschatology, and his use of water in preparing for the day of judgment."[21] In this case, however, the debate has not been fueled by any new texts. The basic arguments had already been refuted by Millar Burrows and Frank Cross in the 1950s. While the Baptist was surely aware of the sectarian settlement near the Dead Sea, he would hardly have been attracted to the regimented life of the community. As Burrows put it in 1955: "if John the Baptist had ever been an Essene, he must have withdrawn from the sect and entered upon an independent prophetic ministry. This is not impossible, but the connection is not so close as to make it seem very probable."[22]

Structural Comparisons

The Teacher's movement and the Jesus movement are both reasonably described as Jewish sects. The former entailed a new covenant, with a clear distinction between those who were in and those who remained outside. The Jesus movement does not seem to have been so clearly defined in the lifetime of the leader, but it was gradually institutionalized after his death. It was inevitable, then, that people would ask how the two movements might be compared.

A classic formulation of the relation between the sect of the Scrolls, identified as the Essenes, and early

Christianity was provided by Frank Moore Cross in 1958. Cross maintained that "the Essenes prove to be the bearers, and in no small part the producers of the apocalyptic tradition of Judaism."[23] (They had been so regarded already in the nineteenth century, long before the Scrolls were discovered, although the Greek and Latin accounts of the Essenes give scant indication of this.) "In some sense," wrote Cross, "the primitive Church is the continuation of this communal and apocalyptic tradition."[24] Like the Essenes, the early Church was distinctive in its consciousness of living already in the end of days. The "eschatological existence" of the early Church, then, its communal life in anticipation of the king-dom, was not a uniquely Christian phenomenon, but had an antecedent in the communities of the Essenes. Both were "apocalyptic communities."

It is in the context of this common eschatological consciousness that the various analogies between the Scrolls and the New Testament must be seen. No-where were these more evident than in the Gospel and Epistles of John, in such phrases as "the spirit of truth and deceit" (1 John 4:6), "sons of light" (John 12:36), or "eternal life" (passim). The affinities of the Johannine literature with the Scrolls had already been noted by Albright, and elaborated by Ray-mond Brown, who wrote a classic commentary on the Gospel in the Anchor Bible series.[25] For Albright and his students (including Cross and Brown) these parallels served to refute the approach of Rudolf Bultmann, who read the New Testament primarily in a Hellenistic context. "These Essene parallels to John and the Johannine Epistles will come as a surprise only to those students of John who have attempted to read John as a work under strong Greek influence," wrote Cross.[26] While he noted that there is no equivalent of the Logos (Word) in the Scrolls, and granted that the Gospel had an elaborate literary history, he concluded: "the point is that John preserves authentic historical material which first took form in an Aramaic or Hebrew milieu where Essene currents still ran strong."[27] Cross was not an especially conservative Christian, although this conclusion, like the positions of the Albright school in general, was attractive to Christians of a conservative bent. More important for Cross was the continuity between early Christianity and Judaism, which was questioned and sometimes denied in German and German-inspired scholarship. Nonetheless, the emphasis on the semitic background of the Johannine literature seems no less one-sided than the alternative Hellenistic approach.

Cross argued that this eschatological consciousness was reflected in the organizational structure of the two movements. He acknowledged from the outset that there is no counterpart in the early Church to the dominance of priests at Qumran, but he regarded the enigmatic "twelve men and three priests" mentioned in 1QS 8:1 as analogous to the twelve apostles. The office of inspector, *mebaqqer* or *paqid*, was thought to parallel the Christian *episkopos*, or bishop.

The boldest analogies drawn by Cross concerned "the central 'sacraments' of the Essene community," baptism and the communal meal. The "baptism of the Essenes" is held to be "like that of John," indicating repentance of sins and acceptance into the eschatological community. Whether in fact initiatory baptism in the Qumran sect was at all comparable to Christian baptism is open to question. Cross argued that the communal meal of the Essenes must be understood as a liturgical anticipation of the messianic banquet, and as such provides a closer parallel to the Christian Eucharist than the Passover meal. Here again Christian practice is taken as the heuristic key to the significance of what is described in the Scrolls, and, again, the analogy is open to question. One Scroll, 1QSa, the Rule of the Congregation, envisages a banquet when the messiah is present, but it does not necessarily follow that every common meal of the sect had eschatological overtones.

But while Cross may have viewed the Scrolls through Christian lenses in some cases, his treatment is distinguished by its sobriety, when compared with the proposals of Dupont-Sommer or

Allegro. The analogies were grounded in the similar eschatological consciousness of the two groups, and in most cases did not require direct Essene influence on early Christianity.

Analogies between the two movements were carried to far greater lengths toward the end of the twentieth century, in the work of maverick scholars, such as Robert Eisenman or the Australian Barbara Thiering. Eisenman contended that the Scrolls provide "nothing less than a picture of the movement from which Christianity sprang in Palestine," or rather "a picture of what Christianity actually *was* in Palestine."[28] He acknowledged that this picture is virtually the opposite of Christianity as it has come down to us, but he claimed it was transformed when Christianity spread to the Gentile world. Both stages of Christianity "used the same vocabulary, the same scriptural passages as proof texts, similar conceptual contexts; but the one can be characterized as the mirror reversal of the other. While the Palestinian one was zealot, nationalistic, engagé, xenophobic, and apocalyptic; the overseas one was cosmopolitan, antinomian, pacifistic—in a word 'Paulinized.' Equally we can refer to the first as Jamesian."[29] He argued that the Teacher of Righteousness was none other than James, the brother of the Lord. For Eisenman, the key to the Scrolls was provided by the coded use of Damascus in the Damascus Document. This he took as a cryptogram for Qumran. When Paul set out for Damascus to persecute the Christians there, he was really setting out for Qumran. Unfortunately, the rest of the scholarly world continues to remain blind to this insight.

Eisenman's suggestion that the Teacher of Righteousness was James the brother of Jesus is hardly the most bizarre theory that has been put forward. An Australian scholar, Barbara Thiering, made John the Baptist the Teacher and cast none other than Jesus as the Wicked Priest.[30] In fairness to Thiering, she did not suggest that Jesus actually was a "wicked priest," only that he was so regarded by the sectarians of the Scrolls. A minor obstacle to this theory is the fact that Jesus was not a priest at all. Eisenman cast Saint Paul in this role, although Paul's priestly credentials are likewise unattested. The theories of Eisenman and Thiering (and a few others) are noted here mainly as curiosities: the strange aberrations to which scholars have been led in their zeal to relate the Scrolls to early Christianity.

A Common Context

While the more ambitious attempts to find in the Scrolls an exact prototype of early Christianity have proved delusional, there is no doubt that the Scrolls shed light on the New Testament in many ways. The two movements overlapped in time, in the same cultural context. They used the same scriptures, and often used them in similar ways. The Scrolls provide a context for debates about such matters as divorce and Sabbath observance, which were of concern to all Jews at the time. Sapiential texts found at Qumran contrast flesh and spirit in ways similar to what we find in the Pauline letters. Another wisdom text contains a list of Beatitudes, which is similar at least in form to the Sermon on the Mount, although the details are quite different. 4QMMT, the treatise on "some of the works of the Law" that sets out the points on which the sect differed from other Jews has been invoked as a parallel for what Paul means by "works of the Law." A document about a heavenly figure named Melchizedek provides a possible background for enigmatic references to Melchizedek in the Epistle to the Hebrews. Examples could be multiplied. Very seldom is it possible to argue that a New Testament writer was influenced by a specific text found at Qumran. The point is rather that both movements drew on the same cultural and religious tradition, and often understood their sacred texts in similar ways, or raised similar questions about them.

If we look at the *Gestalt* of the two movements, however, the differences are at least as striking as the similarities. As Cross argued, both movements expected the coming (or second coming) of a messiah (or messiahs) and believed that actions in this life would determine salvation or damnation in the next. The scenario envisioned in the War Scroll is not so far removed from that of the Book of Revelation. Both envisage a violent confrontation between the forces of good and those of evil, and the eventual destruction of the latter. But the kind of conduct that is thought to lead to salvation in the two movements is fundamentally different. In the Scrolls, the emphasis is on attaining and maintaining a state of purity, and this is achieved by separating from "the men of the pit," which is to say from the rest of society. Jesus, and even more so Paul, in contrast, downplayed the importance of the ritual laws. According to Jesus, it is not what goes into a man that makes him unclean, but what comes out of his mouth. So far from separating from the world of impurity, Paul launched a mission to the Gentiles. Essenism and Christianity were different movements, with different values, even though they arose in essentially the same environment.

Further Reading

An entertaining though sensational account of the controversies surrounding the work of Dupont-

Sommer and Allegro can be found in Michael Baigent and Richard Leigh, *The Dead Sea Scrolls Deception* (London: Jonathan Cape, 1991). Allegro's daughter, Judith Anne Brown, has written a sympathetic account of her father's career in *John Marco Allegro. The Maverick of the Dead Sea Scrolls* (Grand Rapids, MI: Eerdmans, 2005). On the career of Dupont-Sommer see also André Lemaire, "Qumran Research in France," in Devorah Dimant, ed., *The Dead Sea Scrolls in Scholarly Perspective: A History of Research* (STDJ 99; Leiden: Brill 2012)433–47.

The more recent controversies have surrounded the books of Michael Wise, *The First Messiah. Investigating the Savior Before Christ* (San Francisco: Harper, 1999) and Israel Knohl, *The Messiah before Jesus. The Suffering Servant of the Dead Sea Scrolls* (Berkeley: University of California Press, 2000). For an assessment of their theories, see John J. Collins and Craig A. Evans, eds., *Christian Beginnings and the Dead Sea Scrolls* (Grand Rapids, MI: Baker, 2006), 15–44. See also John J. Collins, "The Scrolls and Christianity in American Scholarship," in Dimant, ed., *The Dead Sea Scrolls in Scholarly Perspective*, 197–215. On the Vision of Gabriel, see now Matthias Henze, ed., *Hazon Gabriel. New Readings of the Gabriel Revelation* (SBLEJL 29; Atlanta: Society of Biblical Literature, 2011). For a comprehensive discussion of the messianic texts from Qumran see John J. Collins, *The Scepter and the Star. Messianism in Light of the Dead Sea Scrolls* (2nd ed.: Grand Rapids: Eerdmans, 2010).

Incisive critiques of the books of Eisenman, Thiering, and Baigent and Leigh can be found in Otto Betz and Rainer Riesner, *Jesus, Qumran and the Vatican. Clarifications* (New York: Crossroad, 1994) and Klaus Berger, *The Truth under Lock and Key? Jesus and the Dead Sea Scrolls* (Louisville, KY: Westminster John Knox, 1995). Betz and Riesner also debunk the short-lived theory of José O'Callaghan that a fragment of the Gospel of Mark was found at Qumran. The fragment in question contained only one complete word (*kai* = "and").

For a sober, scholarly, overview of the Scrolls and the New Testament, see Jörg Frey, "Critical Issues in the Investigation of the Scrolls and the New Testament," in Timothy H. Lim and John J. Collins, eds., *The Oxford Handbook of the Dead Sea Scrolls* (Oxford: Oxford University Press, 2010), 517–45.

Map of the Dead Sea Region.

Redrawn from *Beyond the Qumran Community*,
Eerdmans Publishers.

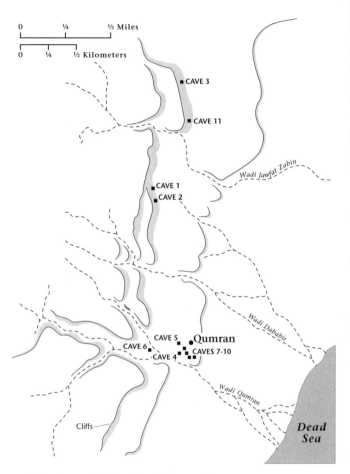

Map showing the location of Qumran Caves.

Redrawn from *Beyond the Qumran Community*.
Eerdmans Publishers.

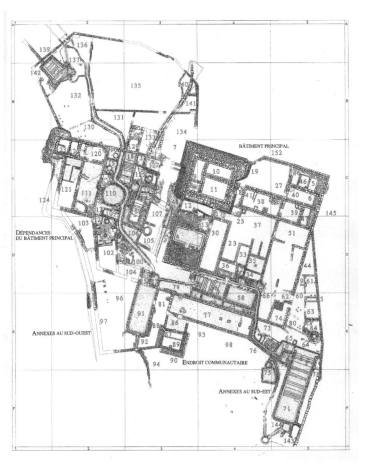

Plan of original fort at Qumran.

Reprinted from Jean-Baptiste Humbert and Alain Chambon, Fouilles de Khirbet Qumrân et de Ain Feshkha (NTOA.SA 1; Fribourg: Editions universitaires, 1994). Courtesy of the École Biblique.

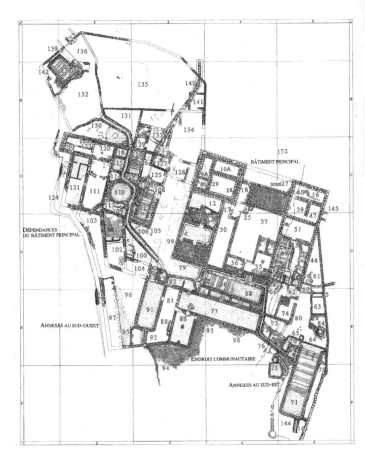

Plan of Khirbet Qumran in period 1b.

Reprinted from Jean-Baptiste Humbert and Alain
Chambon, Fouilles de Khirbet Qumrân et de Ain Feshkha
(NTOA.SA 1; Fribourg: Editions universitaires, 1994).
Courtesy of the École Biblique.

Aerial view of Qumran, looking south.

Reprinted from Y. Hirschfeld, *Qumran in Context: Reassessing the Archaeological Evidence* (Hendrickson, 2004).

Courtesy of the École Biblique.

Cave 1 exterior.

Courtesy of Todd Bolen/BiblePlaces.com.

Cave 4 interior.

Courtesy of Todd Bolen/BiblePlaces.com.

Oriental Research Director Reveals Discovery Of Old Testament Scroll

Four Ancient Documents Including Book Of Isaiah, Unearthed In Jerusalem

From the shelves of an almost forgotten monastery library, the earliest known manuscript of the entire Biblical book of Isaiah from the Old Testament has been discovered in Palestine, it was announced yesterday by Yale Professor Millar Burrows, the Director of the American School of Oriental Research at Jerusalem.

Three other unpublished ancient Hebrew manuscripts have also been brought to light by scholars in the Holy Land. Two of them have been identified and translated while the third still challenges recognition.

First Century BC Origin

The book of the prophet Isaiah was found in a well preserved scroll of parchment. Dr. John C. Trever, a Fellow of the School, examined it and recognized the similarity of the script to that of the Nash Papyrus, believed by many scholars to be the oldest known copy of any part of the Hebrew Bible.

This discovery bears particular significance since its origin is dated about the first century BC. Other complete texts of Isaiah are known to exist only as recently as the ninth century AD.

Found In Monastery Library

All of these ancient scrolls, two in leather and the others in parchment, have been preserved over the centuries in the library of the Syrian Orthodox Monastery of St. Mark in Jerusalem. They were submitted to the American School of Oriental Research for study and identification by the Metropolitan Athanasius Yeshue Samuel and Father Butros Sowmy of the Monastery.

Aside from the book of Isaiah, a second scroll is part of a commentary on the Book of Habakkuk. Habakkuk is a Minor Prophet whose work constitutes one of the books of prophecy of the Old Testament. A third appears to be the manual of discipline of a comparatively unknown little sect or monastic order, possibly the Essenes. The fourth manuscript is still unidentified.

Announcement in the *Yale Daily News*, April 12, 1948.

The Scrolls and Judaism

When the Scrolls first came to light, scholars were mainly impressed by the difference between the worldview they disclosed and that of traditional, rabbinic, Judaism. Most striking was a passage in the Community Rule, which became known as the Instruction on the Two Spirits:

> From the God of Knowledge comes all that is and shall be. Before ever they existed He established their whole design, and when, as ordained for them, they come into being, it is in accord with His glorious design that they accomplish their task without change. The laws of all things are in His hand and He provides them with all their needs.
>
> He has created man to govern the world, and has appointed for him two spirits in which to walk until the time of His visitation: the spirits

of truth and injustice. Those born of truth spring from a fountain of light, but those born of injustice spring from a source of darkness. All the children of righteousness are ruled by the Prince of Light and walk in the ways of light, but all the children of injustice are ruled by the Angel of Darkness and walk in the ways of darkness. The Angel of Darkness leads all the children of righteousness astray, and until his end, all their sin, iniquities, wickedness and all their unlawful deeds are caused by his dominion, in accordance with the mysteries of God . . .

The nature of all the children of men is ruled by these (two spirits), and during their life all the hosts of men have a portion of their divisions and walk in their ways. And the whole reward for their deeds shall be for everlasting ages, according to whether each man's portion in their two divisions is great or small. For God has established the spirits in equal measure until the final age, and has set everlasting hatred between their divisions . . . But in the mysteries of His understanding and in His glorious wisdom, God has ordained an end for injustice, and at the time of the visitation he will destroy it forever. (trans. Vermes)

Here was a dualistic vision of the world without parallel either in the Hebrew Bible or in later rabbinic Judaism. On this account, the presence of evil in the world is due to the fact that God divided the world between good and evil at creation. There was some ambiguity as to whether people are assigned completely to one lot or the other, or rather are given shares in each. But the human condition seemed predetermined in either case.

Another dimension of this dualism was spelled out in the War Scroll, which was also one of the original seven texts found in Qumran Cave 1, which is introduced as "The rule of the war on the unleashing of the attack of the sons of light against the company of the sons of darkness, the army of Belial." The scroll provides instructions for a final war between the opposing dualistic forces. The sons of light are led by the archangel Michael. The sons of darkness include the Kittim,[1] usually identified as the Romans in this text, and are led by Belial, a Satanic figure. The battle is divided into seven phases. Each side prevails in three lots, but in the seventh the mighty hand of God prevails.

Apocalyptic Judaism

The expectation of a final battle between good and evil was not especially new in Jewish tradition. Decisive divine intervention is a standard theme in the prophetic literature. It becomes even more prominent in the apocalyptic literature that came to prominence in the second century BCE. The word *apocalypse* is derived from the Greek word for revelation. An apocalypse is a supernatural revelation, which reveals secrets of the heavenly world, on the one hand, and of eschatological judgment on the other. The Book of Daniel is the only full-blown example of the genre in the Hebrew Bible. It portrays the persecution of the Judeans by the Syrian king Antiochus Epiphanes in the years 167–64 BCE in mythological terms. The gentile kingdoms are portrayed as beasts rising from the sea, imagery drawn from ancient Near Eastern myths. The Judeans, however, are aided by the archangel Michael, described as the prince of Israel, and the holy ones of the Most High, or the angelic host. In the end, the gentile beast is destroyed, and the kingdom is given to a human figure, "one like a son of man," who comes on the clouds, as Yahweh did in the Hebrew Bible. This figure should most probably be identified as the archangel Michael. Daniel also promises that the "wise," who are killed in the time of persecution, will be raised from the dead and will shine with the stars. In apocalyptic idiom, this means that they will become companions to the host of heaven. Daniel is the first clear attestation of the hope for resurrection in the Hebrew Bible.

150   CHAPTER 5

Other examples of apocalyptic literature are found in the books of Enoch, several of which date from the late third or early second century BCE. Enoch had supposedly been taken up to heaven before the Flood, so he was uniquely positioned to reveal both the mysteries of the universe and the course of history. Jewish apocalyptic writings are typically pseudonymous, that is, they are ascribed to people other than their real authors. The supposed authors typically lived in much earlier times, and so they could accurately "predict" the course of history down to the time of the actual authors. This in turn added to the credibility of the real predictions about the events of the end-time. Some of the books of Enoch are concerned with the movements of the stars and with cosmological details that are hidden from humanity, including the abodes of the dead. Others give extensive overviews of history in the form of prophecy, and predict a final judgment. Since Enoch was supposed to have lived long before Moses, the earliest books of Enoch make no overt reference to the Law of Moses, and accordingly seem to represent a kind of Judaism that is very different from the rabbinic tradition.

With the exception of the Book of Daniel, the apocalyptic writings that flourished in the years 200 BCE to 100 CE were not preserved in Jewish tradition. Some survived, usually in translation, in

Christian circles, and even then most of them were unknown for centuries in the Christian West. 1 Enoch, a collection of five books of Enoch, was preserved in Ethiopia, where it was regarded as sacred scripture. At the end of the eighteenth century, it was brought back to England by a Scottish traveler, and in the early nineteenth century it was translated first into English and then into German. A series of other apocalypses were subsequently discovered, in such languages as Syriac and Old Church Slavonic. These writings were not overtly Christian, but neither did they conform to traditional Judaism. Consequently, in the nineteenth century, it was often suggested that they represented the writings of the Essenes, the mysterious sect described in Greek and Latin writings but unknown in Hebrew sources. This suggestion took hold even though the Greek and Latin writers did not ascribe apocalyptic views to the Essenes. Writings that did not fit well in the categories of traditional Judaism were ascribed to a group that was not acknowledged in that tradition, in effect ascribing the unknown to the unknown.

As we have seen already, the belief that the Dead Sea Scrolls were writings of the Essenes arose almost immediately after their discovery, in part because the Roman author Pliny had located an Essene community west of the Dead Sea, and in part because of the similarity between the account of the Essene organization by Josephus and the Community Rule found at Qumran. The fact that the Scrolls contained apocalyptic writings was now taken as confirmation of their Essene origin. "Another argument in favour of the identification of the Jewish New Covenant with the Essenes," wrote Dupont-Sommer, "is the following fact which has considerable implications: it happens that a number of writings whose Essene origin was formerly held by serious scholars to be at least very probable, can be equally connected with the sect of the New Covenant in the light of the recent discoveries."[2] Not only were several copies of the Book of Daniel found at Qumran, but also fragments of other revelations attributed to Daniel. Aramaic fragments of most of the books of Enoch were found, as were Hebrew fragments of the Book of Jubilees, which seems to be cited as scripture in the Damascus Document. Other Aramaic fragments were related to the Testaments of the Twelve Patriarchs. Before the discovery of the Scrolls, it was possible to doubt whether pseudepigraphic writings like 1 Enoch were really Jewish. The Scrolls settled that issue, at least in the case of books like 1 Enoch and Jubilees, which were now attested in their original languages. The Scrolls, then, provided further evidence of a strand of Judaism that was at variance with the tradition taken up by the Rabbis. Its concerns were dominated by eschatological expectation rather than by debates about the exact interpretation of the Law.

Zoroastrian Influence?

The apocalypticism of the Instruction on the Two Spirits and the War Scroll, however, was notably different from that of Enoch and Daniel. It was more strongly dualistic, insofar as humanity was divided ever since creation between forces of light and darkness. The closest parallel to this worldview was found in the teachings of the Persian prophet Zoroaster. Consider the following account of Zoroastrianism by the Greek author Plutarch:

> But they (the Persians) also relate many mythical details about the gods, and the following are instances. Horomazes is born from the purest light and Areimanius from darkness, and they are at war with one another . . . Theopompus says that, according to the Magians, for three thousand years alternately the one god will dominate the other and be dominated, and that for another three thousand years they will fight and make war, until one smashes up the domain of the other.[3]

In this account, the two spirits seem to be primordial. In the hymns of Zoroaster, the Gathas, which are the oldest part of Zoroastrian tradition, the two spirits are the twin children of Ahura Mazda, the wise lord (Horomazes in Plutarch's account), who is the supreme God. The evil spirit is associated with "the Lie." In the Damascus Document, the opponent of the Teacher is known as "the man of the Lie."

Scholars had long suspected that the whole system of thought known as apocalypticism, which appears as a novelty in Judaism in the second century BCE, might be influenced by Zoroastrianism. Besides dualism, Zoroastrianism is characterized by determinism, and by the division of history into periods. Belief in resurrection is attested in Persian religion long before it appears in Judaism. Scholars have been wary of attaching much importance to Zoroastrian influence, however, for two reasons. Many of the most important sources for Zoroastrianism are relatively late (sixth to ninth centuries CE), and while they clearly preserve old traditions, it is often difficult to delineate them. Moreover, very few scholars are trained both in ancient Judaism and in Zoroastrianism. Students of ancient Judaism tend to shy away from texts they cannot read in their original language and whose context they do not understand. Consequently the question of Zoroastrian influence has seldom received the attention it deserves. Nonetheless, the similarity of the two worldviews is evident, and cannot be denied.

It was perhaps unfortunate that the scholar who first demonstrated the affinities of the dualism of the Scrolls with Iranian religion, Karl-Georg Kuhn, had been an active member of the Nazi party, and was tainted with anti-Semitism.[4] After the war, Kuhn tried to distance himself from his Nazi past, without fully acknowledging the extent of his involvement. He was, however, one of the few German scholars of his generation who had been trained in rabbinics, and he had a good philological foundation that included knowledge of Persian. Eventually, in 1964, he was accepted into the Heidelberg Academy of Sciences, on the nomination of Gerhard von Rad and Günther Bornkamm, both of whom had been staunch opponents of the Nazis and members of the confessing church. Whatever Kuhn's earlier sins, and whatever his ideology remained, he became a founding father of German scholarship on the Dead Sea Scrolls, and trained several important scholars (G. Jeremias, H.-W. Kuhn, H. Stegemann). The affinities with Zoroastrianism were not taken to lessen the Jewish character of the Qumran sect. Kuhn wrote that it was, on the one hand, firmly rooted in Jewish tradition, and that its legal observance, or Halakah, was stricter than that of the Pharisees. It relied on the Torah and the Prophets, like other branches of Judaism. On the other hand, its worldview and self-understanding, as disclosed in passages such as the Instruction on the Two Spirits, were fundamentally different from that of the Pharisees.[5]

An Apocalyptic Tradition

Many scholars were reluctant to believe that a Jewish community obsessed with ritual purity and strict observance of the Law of Moses could have been influenced by Zoroastrianism. The idea that it was an apocalyptic community, however, took hold. In the words of Frank Moore Cross: "The Essenes prove to be the bearers, and in no small part the producers, of the apocalyptic tradition of Judaism."[6] Cross recognized that the sect was not the child of a single parent, and he was fully aware that priestly laws of ritual purity were also of fundamental importance. The priestly element resulted from the fact that the traditional Zadokite line had been ousted from the Jerusalem temple before the Maccabean revolt, and was shut out from power when the Maccabees (Hasmoneans) took over the High Priesthood. These displaced priests were thought to be the core of the Qumran sect. The apocalyptic tradition was inherited from the Hasidim of the Maccabean era. These "pious ones" are mentioned only a few times in the books of Maccabees. They were supporters of the Maccabees, but sought to make peace when a High Priest from the traditional family (Alcimus) was appointed. At various times, the Hasidim have been credited with composing the whole range of apocalyptic literature, but there is no indication of this in the few references in the books of Maccabees. In any case, the apocalyptic tradition constituted an alternative in Palestinian Judaism to the Pharisaic-rabbinic tradition, and it was this tradition that would eventually be taken up by Christianity.

All of this had already been claimed for the Essenes in the nineteenth century on the basis of very little evidence. Now the evidence for the apocalypticism of this sect was substantial, not only in the Instruction on the Two Spirits and the War Scroll but also in a host of fragmentary prophetic texts. The view that the Essenes were the bearers of the apocalyptic tradition involved some oversimplification. They were evidently bearers of it, but apocalypticism was not confined to a single movement. Neither is it possible to trace a direct line from the Essenes, or from the apocalyptic tradition, to early Christianity. Christianity, like the Essenes themselves, absorbed influences from more than one quarter.

The apocalyptic view of the Scrolls and the sect has persisted, but it has taken some new forms over the years. In the 1970s and '80s, a suggestion took hold that the Essenes had formed in exile in Babylon, and had returned to Judea in the second century BCE. This theory, put forward especially by Jerome Murphy-O'Connor of the École Biblique, always had a tenuous basis. It depended in part on seeing "Damascus" in the Damascus Document as a code name for Babylon. Eventually, it faded from the discussion. In reaction against this view, however, Adam van der Woude and Florentino García Martínez, of the University of Groningen in the Netherlands, put forward what became known as the "Groningen Hypothesis," reaffirming the view that the sect had developed out of the apocalyptic tradition in Judea. (The theory had some other distinctive features that need not concern us here.) Gabriele Boccaccini, an Italian scholar teaching at the University of Michigan, gave the theory a new twist by defining the tradition as "Enochic Judaism," which in Boccaccini's view posed an alternative to the Zadokite tradition of the High Priestly line, and also to the Mosaic tradition. Both the Groningen Hypothesis and Boccaccini's theory about "Enochic Judaism" rested on valid observations about the continuities between the apocalypticism of the Scrolls and the books of Enoch, but both were reductive in recognizing only a single line of tradition behind the Scrolls.

The Scrolls in Jewish Scholarship

The first two decades of Scrolls scholarship were dominated by Christian scholars, who, naturally enough, were primarily interested in the light the Scrolls might shed on Christianity. Since the bulk of the Scrolls, except for those that had been acquired by Sukenik and Yadin, were under Jordanian control, Jewish scholars did not have access to the fragments, but had to rely on the publications of the official editorial team, and these were frustratingly slow. Consequently, in this period there were few attempts to relate the Scrolls to rabbinic Judaism.

There were exceptions. Saul Lieberman, a great Talmudic scholar at the Jewish Theological Seminary in New York, compared the organization described in the Community Rule with that of the Pharisaic fellowship (*havurah*), which also regulated admission by grades of purity.[7] He also sought to shed light on the Scrolls by considering various allusions to heterodox practices in rabbinic literature.[8] Chayim Rabin went further, and argued that the Qumran group was a diehard Pharisee group trying to uphold "genuine" Pharisaism (as they understood it) against the more flexible ideology introduced by the Rabbis in authority.[9] He looked for his evidence mainly in the Damascus Document, which, unlike the texts from Qumran Cave 1, contained significant discussion of legal interpretations. These ventures, however, were but footnotes to the discussion in this period. As a representative Jewish interpreter of the Scrolls in this period, one can consider Sukenik's son, Yigael Yadin, who published a popular introduction to the corpus in 1957. Like his father before him, Yadin identified the sect with the Essenes. Like most scholars, he argued that the Pharisees were the "Seekers after Smooth Things," the enemies of the sect, who appear in several texts, including the Damascus Document but especially in a commentary on the prophet Nahum. (The Hebrew word for "smooth things," *chalaqot*, is a play on the word for legal rulings, *halakot*.) He inferred this, however, from historical allusions in the biblical commentaries rather than from discussion of biblical interpretations. Yadin was hesitant about the Wicked Priest, but favored identification with Alexander Jannaeus, the Hasmonean king and High Priest in the first quarter of the first century BCE. He noted, correctly, that the Teacher was himself a priest. While he did not pronounce on the causes of the secession of the sect, one might well infer that they involved disputes within the priesthood, as was commonly assumed at the time.

The Arab-Israeli war of 1967, however, had great repercussions. The Scrolls in the Rockefeller Museum in East Jerusalem were now under Israeli control. Even though the Israelis allowed the official editorial team to remain in place for more than two decades, their control over the situation would eventually be decisive for the publication of the corpus. More immediately significant, however, was the recovery of the long document known as the Temple Scroll from the antiquities dealer Kando, by Yadin's soldiers. The publication of this text by Yadin, first in Hebrew in 1977 and then in English in 1983, would be a milestone in the study of the Scrolls.

The Temple Scroll

The Temple Scroll, from Qumran Cave 11, was the longest text recovered from the caves around Qumran. It is presented as a God's revelation to Moses. It begins with the renewal of the Sinai covenant at Exodus 34, and then turns to the building of the Temple in Exodus 35. It takes its name from a lengthy discussion of the structure and furnishings of the Temple, the laws relating to it, and the ritual calendar. It also deals at length with purity rules for the temple and the holy city. The final section of the manuscript is a rewriting of the laws of Deuteronomy 12–23, unrelated to the temple. This last section includes an extensive treatment of the Law of the King from Deuteronomy 17, which restricts the authority of the king even farther than was the case in the biblical text, and subjects him to the authority of the priests.

This text is of exceptional interest for several reasons. The laws are presented as the direct speech of God, using the first person for the speaker. For that reason, some scholars assume that it was intended to replace the traditional Torah, and that it was in effect a new formulation of the Torah. Others doubt this, and suppose that it was meant to supplement and interpret the existing Torah. It could hardly have stood alone as the only version of the Torah. It does not, for example, include the Ten Commandments. Nonetheless, the claim of divine authority is startling.

In part, the Temple Scroll stands in a tradition that goes back to Ezekiel 40–48, which provides a new, ideal layout for the Temple after the Babylonian Exile. (Another text describing a new, ideal, Jerusalem, called, appropriately, "the New Jerusalem Text," was also found at Qumran.) It is a utopian document, not always realistic. It enlarges the size of the temple, so that it would have occupied most of the city of Jerusalem as it then was. It was not, however, a temple for the end of days. It would be replaced in the end-time.

In part, the Scroll is an attempt to harmonize the differences between the various laws in the Torah. In some cases, it goes beyond anything that is written in the traditional biblical text. It does not, in any case, present its new rulings as interpretation of an older Torah. Rather, it presents them as direct revelations from God. In this it differs sharply from other texts found at Qumran, including the Damascus Document. For this reason, also, the majority of scholars have concluded that it was not strictly speaking a sectarian document, but may have been composed before the sect broke away from the rest of Judaism. It does not engage in polemics against the opponents of the Teacher and his movement, in the way that we find, for example, in the Damascus Document. Nonetheless, it is evidently indicative of the tradition from which the Scrolls emerged.

The importance of the Temple Scroll for our story, however, does not lie primarily in its specific teachings, but rather in the prominence that it gives to religious law, especially to laws relating to purity. The date of composition is uncertain—late second or early first century BCE seems probable—but opinions differ. In any case, it shows that Jewish teachers were examining their scriptures to settle questions of religious law a couple of centuries before the rabbinic corpus was compiled. Jewish scholars who had been trained in rabbinic literature now had a corpus of material with similar concerns to work on in the Dead Sea Scrolls. Consequently, there was an upsurge of interest in Halakah, or religious law, in the Scrolls, led by such scholars as Joseph Baumgarten and Lawrence Schiffman. This was a topic that had received only passing attention in the period before 1967.

The Halakic Letter, 4QMMT

Another important text was first revealed to the scholarly world in 1984. This text is known as 4QMMT (*Miqṣat Maʿase ha-Torah*, "Some of the Works of the Law"), also known as the Halakic Letter (or letter about religious law). The text is not actually in the form of a letter, but it seems to be a treatise addressed to a leader of Israel, presumably a High Priest, urging him to accept the writer's interpretation of the Law rather than that of a third party. It concludes by telling him that if he does this, it "will be counted as a virtuous deed of yours, since you will be doing what is righteous and good in His eyes, for your own welfare and for the welfare of Israel." It was presented at the first International Conference on Biblical Archaeology, in Jerusalem, in April 1984, by John Strugnell and Elisha Qimron, a young Israeli scholar whom Strugnell had invited to collaborate with him. In the view of Strugnell and Qimron, this text was "a letter from the Teacher of Righteousness to the Wicked Priest," and it outlined the fundamental issues between sect and the authorities in Jerusalem. One passage stated explicitly: "we have separated ourselves from the multitude of the people . . . and from being involved with these matters and from participating with [them] in all these things."

This text had been noted in the 1950s and labeled 4QMishnaic, because of its manifest similarity to rabbinic law. As such it held little interest for the Christian scholars who were working on the Scrolls, and it was set aside. Only when Israeli scholars were brought into the work of editing was the significance of this text recognized. It contained the most explicit statement found anywhere in the Scrolls about the reasons for which this group had separated itself from the rest of Judean society. Contrary to what had been widely supposed, the sect did not originate in a dispute over the High Priesthood. Rather, it originated in a dispute over the fine points of religious law.

Part of the text dealt with the religious calendar. (There is some dispute as to whether this part of the text is a separate document.) The importance of the calendar for the sect had been recognized early on. In the commentary on Habakkuk, we are told that the Wicked Priest confronted the Teacher on "the Day of Atonement, his Sabbath of rest." Since it is unlikely that the (wicked) High Priest would have staged this confrontation on the day when he himself was celebrating the Day of Atonement (Yom Kippur), it was evident that the two figures observed different cultic calendars. The Scrolls generally attest to a solar calendar of 364 days, whereas the traditional calendar observed in the Temple was a lunar calendar of 354 days. Most scholars agree that calendrical difference was a major reason why the sect had to withdraw from the Temple. The solar calendar is found already in the Temple Scroll and in the Book of Jubilees, both of which are likely to have been written before the sect actually broke off. Differences could simmer for a time, but eventually they led to action.

The main body of 4QMMT, however, deals with some twenty issues bearing on holiness and purity, sacrifice and tithing, forbidden sexual unions, and the like. In each case, the view of the author's group ("we") is contrasted with that of another group ("they"). For example:

> concerning liquid streams: we are of the opinion that they are not pure, and that these

> streams do not act as a separative between im-
> pure and pure. For the liquid of the streams and
> that of the vessel which receives them are alike,
> (being) a single liquid.

So a stream of liquid that is being poured into an unclean vessel is itself impure. From the viewpoint of Christian scholars, and indeed of many modern Jews, many of these issues seem trivial, but for the author and his opponents these matters determined whether the Law was being properly observed.

Several of the issues discussed in 4QMMT appear again in rabbinic literature. The views of the opponents (the "they" group) generally correspond to those of the rabbis, and consequently were those of the rabbis' predecessors, the Pharisees. In some cases, the views espoused in the Scroll correspond to those of the Sadducees. This does not necessarily prove that the author and his group were Sadducees, but that they had a similar approach to the Law. In all cases, the views of the "we" group are stricter than those of their opponents. While 4QMMT does not explain how the author arrived at his positions, the issue was evidently the correct interpretation of the Torah of Moses. The author appeals to the addressee to study the book of Moses and the books of the Prophets and the writings of David. It may well be that the sectarians believed that the true interpretation of the Law had been revealed to them, but if so the revelation came in the course of their study.

There are other indications in the Scrolls that the sect, presumably the Essenes, was at odds with the Pharisees, whom they called "seekers after smooth things." What became clear from 4QMMT was that these disputes about religious law were the primary factor in the separation of the sect, not only from the Pharisees but from the rest of society. In fact, this might already have been inferred from the Damascus Document, which says that God had revealed to the sect the hidden things in which Israel had gone astray. These "hidden things" included the cultic calendar, but also "the three nets of Belial" (CD 4): fornication, riches, and profanation of the Temple. On each of these matters, the sect held a different interpretation of the Law than that of the authorities who controlled the Temple. Again in CD 6 we are told that the members of the new covenant

> shall take care to act according to the exact interpretation of the Law during the age of wickedness . . . They shall distinguish between clean and unclean, and shall proclaim the difference between holy and profane. They shall keep the Sabbath day according to its exact interpreta-

tion, and the feasts and the Day of Fasting according to the finding of the members of the New Covenant in the land of Damascus. They shall set aside the holy things according to the exact teaching concerning them.

It is clear from such passages as this that the exact interpretation of the Law was the raison d'être of the sect. Only when 4QMMT became known, however, was this fact fully appreciated.

4QMMT may also give us a better idea of when this sect broke off from the rest of Judaism. When would a sectarian leader have been likely to appeal to the High Priest to adopt his group's rulings rather than those of the Pharisees? The Pharisees were embroiled in conflicts especially in the early first century BCE. They clashed especially with Alexander Jannaeus, the Hasmonean king who ruled from 103 to 76 BCE. At one point the Pharisees led a revolt against him, on the grounds that he was not fit to be High Priest, and he responded by having some six thousand people killed. He later crucified some eight hundred of his opponents. On his deathbed, however, he advised his queen Salome Alexandra to make peace with the Pharisees. She did so, and entrusted them with the government. According to Josephus,

she permitted the Pharisees to do as they liked in all matters, and also commanded the people to obey them; and whatever regulations, introduced by the Pharisees in accordance with the tradition of their fathers, had been abolished by her father-in-law Hyrcanus, these she again restored. And so, while she had the title of sovereign, the Pharisees had the power. (*Ant* 13. 408–9)

She appointed Hyrcanus II High Priest and he served in that capacity until 67 BCE. He later had a second term from 63 to 40. We should not be surprised if the reversal of royal attitude toward the Pharisees and their rulings provoked a protest from the other sects. This is perhaps the time in Hasmonean history when a High Priest was most likely to take action against people who were contesting the Pharisaic interpretation of the Torah. Josephus says that the Pharisees tried to persuade the queen to kill those who had urged Alexander to put the eight hundred to death, and that they themselves assassinated some of them. We are told in a commentary on Psalms found at Qumran that the Wicked (High) Priest tried to kill the Teacher. This struggle for sectarian hegemony provides a plausible context for the conflict about the Pharisaic interpretation of the Law, when both sides would have sought the endorsement and support of the High Priest. In fact, the great bulk of the historical references in the

Scrolls refer to people and events in the first half of the first century BCE. In contrast, there is no evidence of sectarian conflict in the middle of the second century BCE (the time of Jonathan Maccabee), which had been, and in some circles still is, presumed to be the time of the Teacher and the Wicked Priest.

Mysticism in the Scrolls

We should not suppose, however, that the sectarians were only concerned with religious law. It is evident that they had a dispute with the Temple. The Damascus Document says that "none of those brought into the covenant shall enter the Temple to light His altar in vain" (CD 6). It is not clear whether this means that they should not enter the Temple at all, or only that they should be careful to follow the correct procedures (by sectarian standards). The accounts of Essene practice in this regard are inconsistent. Philo says that they show their piety not by offering sacrifices but by purifying their minds. Josephus, however, says that they send offerings to the temple but use different rituals and are barred from entering the common enclosure. The latter account may be compatible with what we read in the Damascus Document. The Community Rule, however, says nothing about sending offerings to the Temple, but regards the community itself as a substitute for the Temple cult:

> It shall be . . . a house of holiness for Israel, an assembly of supreme holiness for Aaron . . . they shall be the elect of goodwill, who will atone for the Land and pay to the wicked their reward. (1QS 8)

Normally, the Temple cult atoned for the Land by offering the prescribed sacrifices. Since the Temple, in the eyes of the sectarians, was defiled, it fell to them to perform atonement by the way they lived.

There was probably some progression between the situation envisaged in the Damascus Document and that in the Community Rule. The break with the Temple had become more complete.

Separated as they were from the Temple, the sectarians tried to harmonize their lives with the liturgy of the angels in heaven. A text first published in 1959 by John Strugnell, known as the *Songs of the Sabbath Sacrifices*, was originally named an "Angelic Liturgy." It describes, but does not cite, the prayers and blessings pronounced by various angels, e.g., "In the name of his holiness, the seventh of the sovereign Princes shall bless with seven words of his marvelous holiness all the houly founders of knowledge." Presumably, the human community joined in this praise. The Thanksgiving Hymns, or Hodayot, also indicate that the members of the community believed that they were in communion with the angels. The hymnist thanks God, for "thou hast cleansed a perverse spirit of great sin that it may stand with the host of the Holy Ones, and that it may enter into community with the Sons of Heaven" (1QH^a 11). There was, then, a mystical dimension to sectarian life. A hymn appended to the end of the Community Rule says:

> My eyes have gazed on that which is eternal,
> on wisdom concealed from men,
> on knowledge and wise design (hidden) from
>   the sons of men . . .
> God has given them to his chosen ones as an
>   everlasting possession and has caused them
>   to inherit the lot of the Holy Ones.
> He has joined their assembly to the Sons of
>   Heaven
> to be a Council of the Community. (1QS 11)

It is not clear whether members of the sect had mystical practices whereby they experienced ascent to heaven, like later Jewish mystics. (Most of the classic Jewish mystical texts come from the early Middle Ages.) In chapter 4 we had occasion to refer to the so-called Self-Exaltation Hymn, where the speaker boasts of a throne in heaven, and of being reckoned with the gods. The late Morton Smith, who had a somewhat idiosyncratic view of Jesus as a magician and practitioner of occult arts, claimed that this text showed that other Jews around the turn of the era had mystical practices whereby they could ascend to heaven. This, he thought, lent credibility to the view that Jesus was also a mystic. But the figure in the Self-Exaltation Hymn is exceptional in any case, and it is not clear whether he was thought to have made a round trip to heaven during his earthly life. He may be an imaginary figure, such as the eschatological High Priest, or a messiah of some sort. The Thanksgiving Hymns speak of being in communion with the angels. They do not speak of going up to heaven. It may be that the angels were supposed to come down, or that space was irrelevant.

In the apocalypses of Enoch and Daniel, fellowship with the angels in heaven was the reward promised to the righteous after death. In the Dead Sea Scrolls, the sectarians attained this state when they joined the new covenant and participated in its liturgies. Oddly enough, the Scrolls do not speak clearly about resurrection (there are a few disputed passages), although they clearly affirm eternal life for the righteous and damnation for the wicked. They cannot have been unaware of physical death; there was a huge cemetery a stone's throw from the buildings at Qumran. But they seem to have believed that they had made the essential transition when they joined the community. Josephus says that the Essenes believed in immortality of the soul but not resurrection of the body. This was putting the matter in language that Greek and Roman readers would understand. Hebrew speakers did not have the Platonic concept of the soul. Nonetheless, it seems that Josephus was essentially right. The life of the spirit, by which people could mingle with angels even in this life, would continue after death, regardless of the decomposition of the body.

All these texts from the Scrolls are important for the history of Jewish mysticism, even though it is not here as fully developed as it would be centuries later.

Liturgy in the Scrolls

The Scrolls also shed new light on the development of Jewish liturgy. They contain more than a hundred different prayers and numerous religious poems, most of them previously unknown. The Scrolls provide evidence that already before the turn of the era, communal prayer was a religious obligation, at least in some quarters. There were specified times and occasions, and sometimes specified wording. All of this anticipates later rabbinic liturgy, but neither the times nor the rationale for prayer in Scrolls was necessarily the same as what developed later. Here, as in the matter of religious law, we find that the Scrolls address matters that were also of interest to the rabbis centuries later, but that they do not necessarily address them in the same way.

The Scrolls and Common Judaism

The case of liturgical practice may serve to raise an important and difficult question about the significance of the Scrolls. Do these texts tell us only the beliefs and practices of a sect, whether that sect was large or small, isolated or widespread? Or do they give us a window onto what may be called "common Judaism," or concerns that were shared by all Jews of the time, regardless of sectarian affiliation? The texts from Cave 1, which set the tone for discussions of the Scrolls for a long time, were predominantly sectarian. We cannot assume that the Community Rule, or the War Scroll, or even the Hodayot, were typical of anyone outside the "new covenant," or the sect usually identified as the Essenes. As more and more of the corpus of texts from Cave 4 became known, however, it became clear that many of the Scrolls were not especially sectarian in character. An article by Carol Newsom on "'Sectually Explicit' Literature from Qumran,"[10] published in 1990, marked a watershed in this regard. Thereafter, it was increasingly accepted that many texts found among the Scrolls might have been shared by other groups at the time. A collection of non-canonical psalms has no distinctively sectarian features. Several wisdom texts similarly contain no reference to sectarian community structures. Many of the prayers could in principle have been used outside the new covenant. Much of the literature preserved in Aramaic appears to have been composed before the sect developed its separate identity. There is then much in the Scrolls that can be taken as broadly representative of Judaism in this period.

Nonetheless, it remains a tricky question how far the Scrolls can be taken as representative of the Judaism of their day. It remains true that the collection does not include anything that can be identified as Pharisaic, and little if anything that is supportive of the Hasmoneans. (4Q448, A Prayer for King Jonathan, probably Alexander Jannaeus, may date from the time when he was at war with the Pharisees, who were the arch-enemies of the Qumran sect.) The Scrolls may not be the library of the community that lived at Qumran, but they are likely to be the combined libraries of Essene communities, taken to the desert for hiding in a time of crisis. The corpus is to some degree defined by the sect, which was a voluntary association, with its own rite of entry and new covenant. This means that some aspects of Judaism, especially those associated with the enemies of the sect, are likely to be excluded or under-represented. That said, nobody can be sectarian all the time. As we shall see in chapter 6, the Essenes shared a corpus of scriptures with other Jews, even if they interpreted them differently. They also retained some stories, poems, and prayers that did not touch on the divisive issues of the day. Moreover, they attest to certain trends and dominant concerns by the disputes they record, even in cases where the sectarian viewpoint was distinctive. Even if they withdrew from the Jerusalem Temple, they testify to the kinds of debates to which the Temple gave rise in this period.

It is evident that there was considerable diversity in Judaism around the turn of the era, and that it was not a case of contented pluralism. Rival sects and parties hated each other with a perfect hatred, on occasion. Nonetheless, there were also unifying factors—the belief in a single God, shared scriptures, widespread concerns about purity and correct observance, even if these also gave rise to conflict. There was shared ethnic identity too, but it is evident that the true people of God, in the eyes of the sectarians, was not determined by ethnicity alone. It was not sufficient to come from the people of the covenant. It was also necessary for each individual to enter into a new covenant, on the basis of sectarian interpretation.

Apocalypticism and Law

The last thirty years or so have undeniably seen a great shift in the perception of the Scrolls and their importance. That shift was marked emphatically by Lawrence Schiffman, when he entitled his 1994 survey *Reclaiming the Dead Sea Scrolls*.[11] Undeterred by any undue modesty, Schiffman asked: "Is this book revolutionary?" and answered: "In light of the present scrolls mania, especially when it comes to exaggerated claims regarding Christianity, it is indeed revolutionary to propose that the scrolls can be understood only in the context of Jewish history" (p. xxiv). Where the Scrolls had been understood as the product of an apocalyptic movement, a precursor of Christianity, they were now increasingly seen as a record of the debates about the meaning of the Torah that would eventually give rise to rabbinic Judaism.

These two views of the Scrolls, however, should not be seen as antithetical. In fact, both have a good measure of truth. The old emphasis on the apocalyptic aspects of the Scrolls was admittedly one-sided. It can no longer be said with confidence, as it often was, that the dualism of light and darkness was the heart of the sectarian theology. The Instruction on the Two Spirits is not even found in all copies of the Community Rule. Only a few other texts, besides the Community Rule and the War Scroll, reflect this dualistic worldview at all. Moreover, there was a tendency in some Christian scholarship to see apocalypticism as anti-nomian, concerned with cosmic judgment rather than with the details of the Law. We now see that this antithesis is false. It was perfectly possible to live in anticipation of a coming judgment and at the same time immerse oneself in the details of the Law. In fact, it was the conviction that a great judgment was at hand that gave urgency to the need to get the interpretation of the Law right.

The sect described in the Scrolls did not come into being because it believed in the coming of the messiah or the final battle between the sons of Light and the sons of Darkness. It came into being because of disagreements with other Jews on the exact interpretation of the Law, the proper cultic calendar, and the state of the Temple cult. The fact that it had so many irreconcilable differences with other Jews, however, called for explanation. One way of explaining the situation was to suppose that God had hardened the hearts of their opponents, for his own mysterious purposes, and assigned them to the lot of the Spirit of Darkness. It could not be, however, that God would allow error to triumph indefinitely. He must bring an end to it, and soon. Not only must the other Jews who were children of darkness be overthrown, but also the Romans, the Kittim, who were desecrating the land. Hence the need for a final battle in which God would eliminate the forces of evil. It would not be enough that truth and justice prevail in the public order. Individuals must also be punished or rewarded for their deeds. The fact that a judgment is expected, however, does not in itself tell one what conduct is approved. In the case of the Scrolls, right conduct depended on right interpretation of the Law. Early Christianity would have a view of the world that was largely similar, insofar as this world was passing away and would be subject to judgment, but the criteria for the judgment would be quite different, and reflect a different evaluation of the Law, especially its ritual aspects.

Apocalypticism and Torah observance, then, are complementary in the Dead Sea Scrolls. Apocalypticism provides a supporting framework that enables people to endure and persist when the world seems to be against them. True reality is hidden, but it will soon be revealed, and vindicated in a judgment. The criteria for that judgment, however, can vary. In the case of the Scrolls, they were provided by the Torah of Moses, properly interpreted.

Further Reading

On the apocalyptic dimension of the Scrolls, see John J. Collins, *Apocalypticism in the Dead Sea Scrolls* (London: Routledge, 1997).

On the early Enoch literature and its relevance for the Scrolls, see the essays in Gabriele Boccaccini and John J. Collins, *The Early Enoch Literature* (Leiden: Brill, 2007).

On the interpretation of the Scrolls from the perspective of rabbinic Judaism, see Lawrence H. Schiffman, *Reclaiming the Dead Sea Scrolls* (Philadelphia: Jewish Publication Society, 1994); Aharon Shemesh, *Halakah in the Making. The Development of Jewish Law from Qumran to the Rabbis* (Berkeley: University of California Press, 2009).

Several articles pertinent to this chapter may also be found in Lim and Collins, eds., *The Oxford Handbook of the Dead Sea Scrolls*, especially

  M. A. Knibb, "Apocalypticism and Messianism," 403–32;
  J. R. Davila, "Exploring the Mystical Background of the Dead Sea Scrolls," 433–54;

A. de Jong, "Iranian Connections in the Dead Sea Scrolls," 479–500;

A. Shemesh, "Halakhah between the Dead Sea Scrolls and Rabbinic Literature," 595–616; and

D. K. Falk, "The Contribution of the Qumran Scrolls to the Study of Ancient Jewish Liturgy," 617–51.

The Scrolls and the Bible

The initial announcement of the Dead Sea Scrolls in April 1948 had trumpeted the discovery of the earliest known manuscript of the entire Book of Isaiah, and noted that it was older than any other complete Hebrew manuscript of the book by about a thousand years. W. F. Albright promptly predicted that the new discoveries would revolutionize the field of text criticism of the Hebrew Bible. And so they did.

Modern translations of the Hebrew Bible are based on what is known as the Masoretic Text, or MT. The Masoretes were Jewish scribes and scholars, based primarily in the cities of Jerusalem, Tiberias on the Sea of Galilee, and Babylon, in the 7th to 11th century CE. The oldest complete manuscript of the Hebrew Bible is the Leningrad Codex, which was copied about 1008 or 1009 CE. Another important manuscript, the Aleppo Codex, is almost a century older, but it is incomplete.

Besides the Masoretic Text, two other major witnesses to the Hebrew Bible were known before the discovery of the Dead Sea Scrolls.

One was the Samaritan Pentateuch (SP), which is the Samaritan form of the first five books of the Bible (the Torah in Jewish tradition). This was generally regarded as an inferior variant of the Masoretic tradition. It expands the text in some places and tends to harmonize passages that disagree. Its most distinctive aspect is that it claims that Israel's central altar was to be built on Mount Gerizim (the holy mountain of the Samaritans) and that God had chosen Mount Gerizim rather than Jerusalem as the place where his name would dwell.

The other major witness was the Greek translation, popularly known as the Septuagint (LXX), because of a legend that it had been translated by seventy-two Jewish elders at the behest of Ptolemy II (285–247 BCE), who supposedly wanted a copy for the library of Alexandria. These scribes were only supposed to have translated the Pentateuch or Torah, but the name "Septuagint" became attached to the entire Greek Old Testament. The Greek translation was preserved in full in manuscripts from the fourth and fifth centuries CE, which were older than the complete Hebrew manuscripts by several centuries. These manuscripts did not necessarily preserve the original translation exactly. Older forms were occasionally discovered in papyri, or could be detected in the New Testament and other sources. The prevailing opinion before 1948, however, was that when the LXX differed from the MT, this was due to the deficiencies of the translation.

More than two hundred manuscripts of books that we regard as biblical were discovered in the caves around Qumran. The original seven scrolls from Cave 1 included two copies of the Book of Isaiah. One of these, "The Great Isaiah Scroll" or 1QIs^a, differed from the MT in many details, but few of these were significant. The second one, 1QIsa^b, corresponded closely to the traditional text. Initially, the deviations in 1QIsa^a were thought to be a peculiarity of the sect that had preserved it. As more biblical texts were examined, however, the picture grew more complicated.

Different Textual Traditions in the Scrolls

A manuscript of Exodus (4QpaleoExod^m) dated to the middle of the first century BCE (on the basis of paleography) consistently preserves the expansions beyond the MT that are known from the Samaritan Pentateuch. It does not, however, appear to have the specifically Samaritan commandment, to build an altar at Mount Gerizim. (In the Samaritan text, this commandment is inserted in Exodus 20. The Qumran manuscript does not have enough space for the additional commandment at that point.) This suggests that the Samaritan Pentateuch was based on a Jewish text that still circulated in the first century BCE, and differed from it only by the addition of the commandment about Mount Gerizim. A manuscript of the book of Numbers, 4QNum[b], is similar. It also included expansions found in the SP but not in the MT, but it does not contain specifically Samaritan readings. Again, a form of the text that was essentially the same as the Samaritian, but without the special references to Mount Gerizim, seems to have been circulating in Judea in the first century BCE. This form of the text became known as "proto-SP."

The Scrolls also yielded Hebrew texts of some books that correspond to the Septuagint rather than to the MT, and so might be labeled "proto-LXX." The text of Samuel found in three scrolls from Cave 4 consistently agrees with the Greek where the latter disagrees with the MT. One manuscript (4QSam[a]) contains a paragraph that is not found in either the MT or the LXX, but is reflected in the paraphrase of the biblical account by the historian Josephus (*Ant* 6.68–69). An interesting case is provided by the Book of Jeremiah. The Greek text is shorter than the MT by about one-eighth.

Before the discovery of the Scrolls, it was often thought that the translators had simply abbreviated the book. Two small fragmentary manuscripts, however, attest to a Hebrew form of the "short" text underlying the Greek. Both of these manuscripts (4QJer^b and 4QJer^d) are relatively early, dating from the second century BCE. Two other manuscripts of Jeremiah, however, including one early one (4QJer^a, from the early second century BCE), have the long form of the text known from the MT.

The Scrolls have provided plenty of evidence that the traditional text of the Hebrew Bible, the MT, or rather the proto-MT, was well known already in the last centuries BCE. But it was not the only form of the text. Different editions circulated side by side, much as different English translations of the Bible circulate in the modern world. (The textual differences in the Scrolls, however, are considerably more substantial than the differences between modern translations, at least in some cases.) The Book of Exodus was part of the Torah of Moses, and was certainly regarded as authoritative. But it was the book that was authoritative, rather than a particular form of the text, just as in a modern context the authority of the book does not depend on the wording of any one translation. For Christians brought up to believe in verbal inspiration, this may come as something of a shock. The actual words of the

Bible, even the words of the Pentateuch or Torah, were not definitively fixed in the time of Christ.

Local Texts

In 1955, William F. Albright, the leading authority on most things relating to the Hebrew Bible and the ancient Near East, attempted to bring order to the evidence for textual fluidity by proposing a theory of local texts.[1] The proto-MT would have developed in Babylonia, the proto-LXX in Egypt, and the proto-Samaritan in Palestine. This theory was refined and propagated by Frank Moore Cross.[2] The underlying assumption was that different forms of the text could only have developed in distinct locations. Nonetheless, the evidence for the three distinct forms of the text was all found together in a cave at Qumran.

Not all scholars believed that the evidence could be so neatly organized. No two manuscripts are actually identical. Dividing them into groups, or "textual families," always involves a measure of subjectivity in deciding where to draw the lines. Where Albright and Cross saw the distinct contours of forests, others saw only trees, some clustered to be sure, but in great variety. Emanuel Tov, who eventually supervised the publication of most of the Scrolls, but had begun his career as a text critic and student of Frank Cross, argued that some texts should be recognized as "non-aligned," meaning that they should not be categorized as proto-MT, proto-SP, or proto-LXX.[3] Others would argue that no text is ever "non-aligned," but that the relationships between them are too complex to reduce to textual families.

Moreover, *sociological* context may be more important than *geographical* context. Eventually, the MT was preserved in Jewish communities, the LXX by Christians, and the SP by Samaritans. It may be that the different text-types were also developed by different groups, although we cannot now identify them. Many scholars think that the textual tradition that became the MT was that of the Pharisees, the precursors of the Rabbis. If the Scrolls can be taken as evidence for preferences of one particular sect—the Essenes—however, it would seem that they had no clear preference for one textual tradition. Scholars have increasingly come to think that in this respect at least the Scrolls are broadly typical of Palestinian Judaism in the period before the revolts against Rome, and that there was no officially standard text in this period.

A Move Toward Standardization?

In 2002, when the process of publishing the Scrolls was nearing completion, an attempt was made to provide an overview of the corpus in a way that had not previously been possible.[4] This included a chronological index of the texts—an attempt to arrange them by the date on which they were copied.[5] These dates are not beyond dispute: they were assigned by the various editors on the basis of paleography, or handwriting. Not all editors necessarily used the same criteria, or were equally competent. But the list at least gives an impression of which texts were earlier and which were later. If we may take this list as a guide, there was great variety in the text types of the biblical manuscripts until the middle of the first century BCE. Some proto-MT manuscripts are also early, even from the second century BCE. They become more numerous, however, in the second half of the first century BCE. In the first century CE, the number of manuscripts that are not proto-MT decreases steadily. All the manuscripts found at Qumran are assumed to date before 70 CE. A few biblical manuscripts from the period after 70 were found at Murabbaʿat. These are all of the proto-MT type.

While the dating of these manuscripts is somewhat tentative, they do appear to show a trend toward adopting the proto-MT tradition as the standard form of the text, in the first century CE. The Scrolls give no clue, however, as to how or why this came about. There is nothing to indicate that the sectarians ever had a distinctive form of the text. In principle, they seem to have used those forms of the text that were current at the time. Since the proto-MT form of the text prevailed after 70, it is safe to say that it was not especially associated with the Essenes. It may have been preferred by the Temple scribes, or perhaps by the Pharisees, but this is mere conjecture.

The most notable lesson from the Dead Sea Scrolls about the text of the Hebrew Bible, however, is that prior to the turn of the era there were many forms of it in circulation.

The Phenomenon of Rewritten Scriptures

The fluidity of the biblical text is related to another phenomenon that figures prominently in the Dead Sea Scrolls. Beginning about the late third or second century BCE, it became popular to write paraphrases of biblical books, often introducing new ideas in the process. These rewritings could serve various purposes. Some Jews in Alexandria, writing in Greek, tried to recast parts of the biblical narratives in the Greek genres of epic or tragedy. The *Jewish Antiquities* of Josephus was an attempt to present the entire biblical record as history. The Aramaic *Genesis Apocryphon*, one of the initial scrolls found in Qumran Cave 1, is an entertaining account of some episodes of Genesis that included an expanded description of the beauty of Sarah, wife of Abraham. In other cases, the rewritten scriptures lay claim to the status of revelation, and their relation to the traditional scriptures becomes problematic.

A particularly clear case of rewritten scripture is provided by the Book of Jubilees. This text was preserved in full in Ethiopic, and was regarded as scripture in the Ethiopian church. Fragments of the Hebrew original were found at Qumran. It is believed to date from the second century BCE. It is a paraphrase of Genesis and the first part of Exodus, with a definite theological message. The laws of Moses were already observed by the patriarchs in Genesis, and the true calendar was the solar one, with 364 days. Jubilees, however, sometimes refers to what had been revealed in "the first Torah," and so it clearly was not trying to replace the traditional Torah, only to supplement and interpret it. Nonetheless, it is cited as an authoritative text in the Damascus Document, and it later became canonical in the Ethiopian church.

The situation was different with the Temple Scroll, which we have already discussed in chapter 5. This too was a rewriting of a part of the Torah, but in this case there was no acknowledgment of "the first Torah," and the reformulated laws were presented as divine revelation. The Temple Scroll does not repeat everything that is found in the laws of the Pentateuch. It does not, for example, include the Ten Commandments. But for the matters it does address (largely matters relating to the purity of the Temple, but also some laws from Deuteronomy), it claims the highest imaginable authority. When it was first published, some scholars thought that this was "the Torah of Qumran," the special sectarian edition of the Law. In fact, however, citations of the Torah in the Scrolls generally conform to the traditional text, not to the Temple Scroll. If the authors of the Temple Scroll wanted it to be accepted as the official Torah, they failed. Nonetheless, several copies of it were preserved among the Scrolls.

An even more problematic case is that of a text known as 4QReworked Pentateuch. This title refers to a set of five fragmentary manuscripts that were originally thought to pertain to the same text.[6] They are now regarded as five separate compositions. Compared with the MT, all five show major expansions. For example, the "song of Miriam" in Exodus 15:21 was filled out in a way that has no parallel in the MT. Material is also rearranged in some cases. There is no indication, however, that this material records a new revelation. The differences over against the MT are typical of the proto-Samaritan tradition. Increasingly, scholars have come to regard these fragments not as "Reworked Pentateuch" or "Rewritten Bible," but simply as a variant edition of the Book of Exodus. Here again it seems that scribes were not bound by any official, standard, form of the text in the last centuries before the turn of the era.

A Biblical Canon?

Strictly speaking, it is anachronistic to speak of a Bible at Qumran or in the Dead Sea Scrolls. The Bible as we know it had not yet taken its final shape. That did not happen until the late first century CE, or possibly later. But there is no doubt that sacred scriptures were enormously important for the life of the sect, and even that the interpretation of those scriptures was its raison d'être.

Several passages in the sectarian rule books testify to the importance of the Law of Moses. In CD 15, the members of the new covenant are enrolled "with the oath of the covenant which Moses made with all Israel, the covenant to return to the Law of Moses with a whole heart and soul." Elsewhere, the same document cites Numbers 21:18: "the well which the princes dug, which the nobles of the people dug with the staff," and explains it as follows: "the well is the Law, and those who dug it were the converts of Israel." The staff is "the interpreter of the Law," who defines how the Law is to be observed. The manner in which the Law was studied is prescribed in 1QS 6:

> and where there are ten, there shall never lack
> a man among them who will study the Law,
> day and night, one relieving the other. And the
> Many shall be on watch together for a third of
> each night of the year in order to read the book,
> explain the regulation and bless together.

Even the quotation of Isaiah 40:3, "in the desert, prepare the way of the Lord," is interpreted as

> this is the study of the Law which he commanded through the hand of Moses, in order
> to act in compliance with all that has been revealed from age to age, and according to what
> the prophets have revealed through his holy
> spirit. (1QS 8)

The Law, in these passages, is the Torah of Moses, the first five books of the Bible, or Pentateuch. This was evidently the touchstone for proper religious life. The prophets were also important.

These scriptures were not peculiar to the sect. They were the scriptures of all Israel. When a sectarian leader appealed to the High Priest in 4QMMT, he wrote:

> We have written to you that you may study the book of Moses and the books of the Prophets and David.[7]

"David" here means the Book of Psalms, which was often read as a prophetic text. This passage in 4QMMT shows that the sectarians accepted the same basic scriptures as the High Priest, and even as their opponents, the Pharisees. The Law and the Prophets, or the Law, the Prophets, and David, were the scriptures shared by all Judeans in the first century BCE.

The traditional Hebrew Bible contains a third category besides the Law and the Prophets—the Writings. (The Hebrew Bible is sometimes referred to as the TANAK, for the Torah [Law], Neviim [Prophets], and Kethuvim [Writings].) The earliest evidence for this division is found in the Greek translation of the Book of Ben Sira, by his grandson, in the late second century BCE. In the prologue to the translation, the grandson says:

> So my grandfather Jesus, who had devoted himself especially to the reading of the Law and

the Prophets and the other books of our ances-
tors . . . was himself also led to write something
pertaining to wisdom and instruction.

This passage has often been taken as evidence that
the three-part canon of scripture was already established by the end of the second century BCE. In
fact, it indicates that the Law and the Prophets
were well-established categories. "The other books,"
however, was an open-ended category of edifying
literature. Ben Sira himself fancied that he could
contribute to it.

When 4QMMT was published, some schol-
ars thought it provided evidence for a three-part
canon: the Law, the Prophets, and David. A fragmentary mention of "generations" was sometimes
read as a reference to the books of Chronicles, and
thought to imply that the whole Hebrew canon
as we know it was included. This is not convincing, however. It is clear that both the sect and its
opponents regarded the Torah, the Prophets, and
Psalms, in some form, as authoritative, but that was
the extent of the shared scriptures in the early first
century BCE.

The word "canon" means measuring stick. It was
applied to the scriptures by the Christian Church
Fathers. There was no such term in Hebrew, but the
idea of a corpus of authoritative scriptures was cer-

tainly present by the time of the Dead Sea Scrolls. It has often been pointed out that every book of the Hebrew Bible except the Book of Esther has been found at Qumran, with the implication that they were all recognized as authoritative scriptures. But the situation is somewhat more complicated than this.

A huge corpus of supposedly revelatory texts was found at Qumran. It is difficult to know how these texts were regarded by the people who read them. Some texts (such as the books of Enoch) that did not become part of the traditional Hebrew canon were preserved in multiple copies. Some books that did become canonical, such as Chronicles, are barely represented. If we judge by the number of copies preserved, such books as 1 Enoch and Jubilees were more important to the sectarians than Proverbs or Qoheleth.

While it is clear that the Law and the Prophets were canonical, it is not certain what these were thought to contain. Would the Temple Scroll have been regarded as part of the Law of Moses? or would even Jubilees have been so regarded, although it clearly distinguishes itself from "the first Torah"? The Book of Daniel is classified with the Writings rather than the Prophets in the traditional Bible. Yet Daniel is called a prophet in the Scrolls (11QMelchizedek). Various prophetic, or quasi-prophetic, writings are preserved (e.g., 4QPseudo-Ezekiel; 4QPseudo-Daniel). Were these accepted as genuine prophetic writings?

One way of addressing this problem is to note which books are cited, and which ones have commentaries devoted to them. A distinctive sectarian kind of commentary, called *pesher*, to which we will return below, has been found for Isaiah, Hosea, Micah, Nahum, Habakkuk, Zephaniah, and Psalms. There are also fragments of commentaries on Genesis and on the prophet Malachi. No one would suggest, however, that the prophets Jeremiah and Ezekiel were not authoritative because we do not have commentaries on them. Several other texts are cited on occasion, but even these citations do not necessarily give us a complete picture. The collection of writings that enjoyed some degree of authority is open-ended.

The uncertainty about the scope of the authoritative scriptures can be illustrated by the debate about a manuscript of the Psalms, 11QPs^a, which was published by James Sanders in 1965.[8] This scroll contains thirty-nine psalms also found in the MT, as well as ten additional compositions, including a prose account of "David's Compositions." Some of the additional psalms were previously known from the Greek and Syriac Bibles. Others were not. The order of the familiar psalms is different from that of the MT. Two other manuscripts from Qumran seem to have had the same edition as 11QPs^a, but none of the Scrolls unambiguously supports the order of the MT.

Sanders considered 11QPs^a a biblical scroll. Several prominent scholars, including Patrick Skehan of the official editorial team and Shemaryahu Talmon of the Hebrew University, rejected this suggestion, and argued that this was *only* a liturgical compilation. Each side was partially correct, and partially wrong. In this period, there was no such thing as a biblical manuscript of the psalms. All manuscripts of the psalms were "liturgical collections," including the MT edition. But Sanders was right that 11QPs^a was as authoritative as any other collection at that time. There was no official "canonical" edition from which this manuscript could be said to deviate.

In short, the Dead Sea Scrolls attest to a collection of authoritative scriptures that overlaps to a great degree with the later Bible of the rabbis. It was substantially the same in the Torah and the Prophets, although the status of some works, such as the Temple Scroll and Jubilees, is unclear. The Essenes may have had a larger collection of prophets and other writings than the authorities in the Jerusalem Temple or the Pharisees; they did not have a smaller one. The whole category of "Writings" was ill-defined. It is clear that the sectarians valued many writings that claimed to be revelatory, but that were not included in the rabbinic Bible. Only in the period after 70 CE, in the writings of the historian Josephus and in 4 Ezra, an apocalypse written about 100 CE, do we find authoritative sacred writings limited to a specific number. Josephus says that twenty-two books were properly accredited (*Against Apion*, 1.39). 4 Ezra gives the number as twenty-four (probably the same books counted differently), but it also refers to seventy hidden books which contained even greater wisdom. It may be that Josephus's list of twenty-two books had been defined better before 70 CE, either by the Pharisees or by the Temple authorities, but there is no evidence of such a limitation in the Scrolls, and it was evidently not universally accepted.

The Interpretation of Scripture

The received scriptures are interpreted in the Dead Sea Scrolls in manifold ways.

The first batch of Scrolls from Qumran Cave 1 contained a commentary on the prophet Habakkuk of a type that was previously unknown, which became known as *pesher*, from the word it uses for "interpretation." This was a formal commentary, which typically cited a verse or two, and then gave an interpretation, introduced by the words "its interpretation (*pesher*) concerns . . ." Typically, the words of the prophet were taken to refer to events in the commentator's own time, which itself was understood as the end-time of history. Habakkuk's prophecy refers to the Chaldeans, or Babylonians, who invaded and destroyed Jerusalem in the early sixth century BCE. For the commentator, the Chaldeans were identified as the Kittim, or westerners, and clearly refer to the Romans, who invaded Judea and conquered Jerusalem in 63 BCE under the general Pompey. There was evidently a principle of analogy at work here. "Babylon" would often serve as a code name for Rome in later apocalyptic writings, including the Book of Revelation, because both destroyed Jerusalem. Other references in Habakkuk were taken to refer to the history of the sectarian movement. For example, when Hab 1:13 says that the wicked swallows up one more righteous than he, this is interpreted as a reference to the "man of the Lie" and the Teacher of Righteousness. A reference to "the arrogant man" who seizes wealth without halting, in Hab 2:5–6, is taken as a reference to "the Wicked Priest." Hab 2:15: "Woe to him who causes his neighbours to drink; who pours out his venom to make them drunk that he may gaze on their feasts," is taken to refer to the Wicked

Priest who disrupted the Teacher's observance of the Day of Atonement.

The assumption underlying this kind of commentary is stated explicitly in a comment on Hab 2:1–2: "Write down the vision and make it plain upon the tablets, that he who reads may read it speedily":

> God told Habakkuk to write down that which would happen to the final generation, but He did not make known to him when time would come to an end. And as for that which He said, *That he who reads may read it speedily*: interpreted, this concerns the Teacher of Righteousness, to whom God made known all the mysteries of the words of His servants the Prophets.

In short, the prophecies of scripture were coded speech, which did not refer to their own time but to the end-time, which had now arrived. The key to the code was given to the Teacher. It is unlikely that the Teacher himself was the author of all the pesher commentaries, but they reflect a way of reading prophecy that he had presumably taught to his followers. This mode of interpretation has little in common with the methods of modern scholarship. It pays little attention to literary context, and scarcely any to historical context, although it does seek to relate the text to other biblical passages. In some respects, it is comparable to the ways in which

Fundamentalist preachers interpret Scripture in the modern world.

When Cave 4 was discovered, it became apparent that this commentary on Habakkuk was not unique, but was rather an example of a genre. Similar commentaries on several other prophetic books, and also on Psalms, were found. One of these, the *Pesher* on Nahum, referred clearly to the Hasmonean king Alexander Jannaeus, as "the Lion of Wrath who hangs men alive," and mentioned a Syrian king Demetrios by name.

These commentaries, dating from the first century BCE, are the oldest biblical commentaries that are substantially preserved. (An Alexandrian Jew named Aristobulus had written a commentary on the Torah in the second century BCE, but it is known only from a few quotations.) The *Pesharim* are a distinctive product of the sect, presumably the Essenes, as can be seen from their focus on events of consequence for the history of the movement. A similar way of interpreting prophetic texts can be found in other texts that are not formal commentaries. Some of these became known as "thematic" *pesharim*, which strung together passages from different biblical books and related them to a common topic, in contrast to the "continuous pesharim," or sustained commentaries on individual books. For example, a text called the Florilegium (4Q174) strings together passages from 2 Samuel 7 and Psalms 1 and 2. Another text, called the Melchizedek Scroll, from Cave 11, begins with a citation from Leviticus 25 about the Jubilee, and goes on to cite a range of texts from the Psalms and Prophets and relates them to the final Day of Atonement at the end of history, when a heavenly priest, Melchizedek, would execute judgment. These texts relate the prophetic texts to the end of history, but do not necessarily take them as predictions of the history of the sect. In fact, this way of interpreting scripture was also used in other circles. We find it already in the Book of Daniel, where Jeremiah's prophecy, that Jerusalem would be desolate for seventy years, was taken as a prophecy of the duration of history, and the seventy years were taken as seventy *weeks* of years, or 490 years, from the destruction of Jerusalem by the Babylonians.

Initially, the pesher commentaries aroused great interest for two reasons. On the one hand, they were arguably the main source of evidence for the history of the sectarian movement. On the other, they filled in the context of the way scripture is used in the New Testament.

To be sure, the historical information provided by these commentaries is obscure. With the exception of King Demetrios in the Nahum *Pesher*, key players were identified only by nicknames—Teacher of Righteousness, Liar, Wicked Priest. Since the latter was presumably a High Priest, he offered the best hope for identification. A consensus developed in the 1950s that he was one of the brothers of Judas Maccabee, probably Jonathan, who became High Priest in 152 BCE, although his brother Simon was also suggested. Two High Priests from the first century BCE, Alexander Jannaeus and Hyrcanus II, were also proposed early on, the latter being favored by Dupont-Sommer. In recent years, the latter suggestion has been revived, and the question of the date of the Teacher has been reopened.

Some scholars have objected to the use of the Pesher commentaries as historical sources. They point out, reasonably, that the comments are constrained by the biblical text that they happen to be expounding. The commentators use various exegetical techniques to arrive at their exposition. Often they cite other scriptural passages to make their point. They do not report history in any straightforward sense. Even when they do allude to historical events, they are usually concerned to show that God either has already or will shortly vindicate the sect and confound their enemies. All this is undoubtedly true, but these commentaries still remain an important historical source. The Book of Habakkuk does not mention a priest at all. Nonetheless, the Wicked Priest is a major character in the pesher. His existence was not deduced from the biblical text. In short, the commentaries do refer to historical characters and events, and while their identification may be difficult, it is a legitimate topic of research.

The early Christians did not write Pesher commentaries in the precise fashion that we find in the Scrolls. They did, however, appeal to Scripture to explain the things that were happening in their time, under the assumption that the end of history was at hand. Very often in the New Testament we find fulfillment formulae: "Then was fulfilled what had been spoken through the prophet." Sometimes the referent of a prophetic passage is identified, in a way that is quite similar to a pesher. When John the Baptist is introduced in Matthew 3:1–3 we are told: "This is the one of whom the prophet Isaiah spoke when he said, 'the voice of one crying out in the wilderness, prepare the way of the Lord.'" Sometimes we find passages from the prophets and psalms strung together in the manner of the continuous pesharim. For example, the first chapter of the Epistle to the Hebrews cites Psalm 2, followed by a verse from 2 Samuel 7, and then several other passages from the Psalms. Psalm 2 and 2 Samuel 7 were also juxtaposed in a text known as the *Florilegium* from Qumran (4Q174). The early Christians shared various exegetical traditions with the Scrolls, and sometimes combined biblical passages in similar ways.

The comparison of the ways in which Scripture is used in the Scrolls and in early Christianity remains a fertile area for exploration. In recent decades, however, the focus has shifted increasingly to analogies between the Scrolls and later, rabbinic, exegesis, especially midrash. When the Pesher commentaries were originally published, there was a debate as to whether they should be classified as "midrash." The word "midrash" is actually used in the *Florilegium* (4Q174) to describe the interpretation of Psalm 1. In rabbinic tradition, however, midrash became the name for a kind of commentary, which resembles the peshers in some respects but differs from them in others. The midrash is not typically concerned with identifying events or with eschatological judgment.

The pesher was not the only kind of biblical interpretation in the Scrolls. We have already had occasion to touch on the question of legal interpretation, which was employed especially on the laws of the Pentateuch. The whole phenomenon of "rewritten scriptures" was an exercise in interpretation. In this case, the interpretations are worked into the rewritten narrative. Pesher-like explanations of what a given phrase means can also be found in other genres. One fragmentary text from Cave 4, 4Q252, retells selected passages from Genesis in order to resolve problems in the biblical text. The Blessing of Jacob, in Genesis 49, however, was read as a prophetic text. When this fragment was first published it was dubbed "*Pesher* on Genesis" because of the way in which the biblical text was decoded. It later became clear that this passage was atypical of the text as a whole, which is closer to the kind of writing we know as rewritten scriptures. Some texts use Scripture without citing it explicitly at all. The Thanksgiving Hymns (Hodayot) are full of allusions to biblical texts. A large wisdom text (4QInstruction), which is not necessarily a sectarian composition, offers an account of the nature of humanity that clearly depends on the creation stories in Genesis. This is also true of the "Instruction on the Two Spirits" in the Community Rule.

While the pesher commentaries are distinctly sectarian, many of their techniques of interpretation can be paralleled more broadly in other Jewish writings of the time. The phenomenon of rewritten scripture was very widespread and not at all peculiar to the sect. Here again the Scrolls have some distinctive features, but also shed light on "common Judaism" as it existed around the turn of the era.

Further Reading

A comprehensive study of the import of the scrolls for the Bible, including the New Testament, can be found in James C. VanderKam, *The Dead Sea Scrolls and the Bible* (Grand Rapids, MI: Eerdmans, 2011).

On the significance of the Scrolls for textual criticism of the Hebrew Bible, see Emanuel Tov, *Textual Criticism of the Hebrew Bible* (Minneapolis: Fortress, 1992), and Ronald S. Hendel, "Assessing the Text-Critical Theories of the Hebrew Bible after Qumran," in Lim and Collins, eds., *The Oxford Handbook of the Dead Sea Scrolls*, 28–302.

On the phenomenon of rewritten scriptures, see Sidnie White Crawford, *Rewriting Scripture in Second Temple Times* (Grand Rapids, MI: Eerdmans, 2008), and Molly M. Zahn, "Rewritten Scriptures," in Lim and Collins, eds., *The Oxford Handbook of the Dead Sea Scrolls*, 323–36.

On the significance of the Scrolls for the formation of the canon of Scripture, see Timothy H. Lim, "Authoritative Scriptures and the Dead Sea Scrolls," in *The Oxford Handbook of the Dead Sea Scrolls*, 303–22.

On biblical interpretation in the Scrolls, see Moshe Bernstein, "The Contribution of the Qumran Discoveries to the History of Early Biblical Interpretation," in Hindy Najman and Judith H. Newman, eds., *The Idea of Biblical Interpretation: Essays in Honor of James L. Kugel* (Leiden: Brill, 2004), 215–38.

The Battle for the Scrolls

The publication of the Scrolls had slowed to a trickle after 1960. By then, several members of the editorial team had dispersed—some, like Cross and Strugnell, to demanding academic positions. By 1972, some signs of impatience were beginning to appear. At the behest of Geza Vermes, professor of Jewish Studies at Oxford, Oxford University Press demanded a timetable for publication. Only Cross, Strugnell, and Skehan responded, all promising to submit their material by 1976. The promises went unfulfilled, which is not to say that they were not made in all sincerity. In 1977, on the thirtieth anniversary of the first discoveries, Vermes stated famously that "unless drastic measures are taken at once, the greatest and most valuable of all Hebrew and Aramaic manuscript discoveries is likely to become the academic scandal *par excellence* of the twentieth century."[1]

By this time, de Vaux was dead, and had been replaced as editor-in-chief by Pierre Benoit O.P., a gentle New Testament scholar who was ill-fitted for the job. He resigned in 1985, two years before his death. At this point he was replaced by John Strugnell. Strugnell's tenure as editor-in-chief, which lasted a mere five years, ushered in the most turbulent period in the biography of the Dead Sea Scrolls.

John Strugnell

Strugnell had been something of a child prodigy when he became the youngest member of the editorial team in 1954, at the tender age of twenty-four. He had a remarkable facility for ancient languages. He was reputed to be second only to Milik in deciphering fragmentary texts. He had a distinguished career as a professor, first at Duke University from 1960 to 1967 and then at Harvard University, where he trained many of the leaders of the emerging field of "intertestamental literature," which morphed into "Second Temple Judaism" in the latter part of the twentieth century. He had less facility, however, for the practical things of life (such as driving a car). While his speech was elegant, his appearance was often disheveled. Despite his phenomenal learning, he was never the sole author of a book. His reluctance to publish was largely a result of perfectionism. His longest publication before 1985 was a scathing review of a volume of fragments from Cave 4, *Discoveries in the Judaean Desert*, volume 5, which had been published by Allegro in 1968. The review ran to more than a hundred pages. Already by the early 1970s, it was apparent that Strugnell suffered from manic depression, compounded by alcoholism. His condition deteriorated when his marriage ended in 1974.

He might seem, then, to have been an odd choice for the role of editor-in-chief of a daunting project in 1985, but unless the Israel Antiquities Authority had been willing to go outside the circle of the original editors, the options were limited. Frank Moore Cross, at the height of a very distinguished career as Hancock Professor of Hebrew and Other Semitic Languages at Harvard, where he supervised more than one hundred doctoral dissertations, did not want the job. J. T. Milik, who by this time had left the priesthood and married, also suffered from alcoholism, and was arguably in worse shape than Strugnell. (Milik was eight years older.) Whatever Strugnell's problems, he knew the corpus of the Scrolls intimately. Nonetheless, in view of his own inability to publish, he was hardly the person to expedite the publication of the Dead Sea Scrolls.

He did, however, try. It was he who first invited Israeli scholars to collaborate in the editing process. His collaboration with Elisha Qimron led to the momentous presentation of 4QMMT in 1984, which revolutionized the study of the Scrolls. (He had enlisted the cooperation of Qimron already in 1979.) Other Jewish scholars who were now brought into the process included Devorah Dimant, of Haifa University, Joseph Baumgarten, of Baltimore Hebrew College, and Emanuel Tov, who would eventually become editor-in-chief. (Other, non-Jewish, scholars were also added to the team, notably James VanderKam in 1989.) Only one volume of the *Discoveries in the Judaean Desert* appeared during Strugnell's tenure (only 2 volumes had appeared in the much longer tenure of his predecessor), but his modest expansion of the editorial team would eventually bear fruit.

Somewhat ironically, the presentation of 4QMMT, which was one of Strugnell's major contributions to the study of the Scrolls, was one of the factors that led to the upheavals at the end of his tenure. Prior to this disclosure, it was possible to believe that all the most important texts had already been published. Now it was evident that this was not so, and the scholarly community, and also the media, became increasingly insistent that the rest of the corpus be made public.

Another development of the 1980s which was intended to advance the cause, and actually did so, also added to popular discontent. Cross and Strugnell began to assign unpublished works to their graduate students at Harvard, as topics for their dissertations. (This development happened long after my own time as a student at Harvard. There was not even a course on the Scrolls when I studied with Strugnell there in 1969–72.) These students did excellent work, and several went on to become leading scholars in the field (Carol Newsom, Eileen Schuller, Sidnie White Crawford, among others). A few other very young scholars from other institutions were also entrusted with editing texts. This advanced the publication of the texts, but it also bred resentment, not only among senior, well-respected, scholars like Geza Vermes but also among scholars like Norman Golb and Robert Eisenman, who suffered the added frustration that their views were not respected in the scholarly community. In 1989, Eisenman and Philip Davies, a prominent but contentious British scholar, sent a well-publicized request to Strugnell to see certain scrolls. The request was denied, and the denial was also well-publicized. Hershel Shanks, the editor of *Biblical Archaeology Review* (*BAR*), now regularly devoted the pages of his journal to a persistent campaign for the release of the Scrolls. Strugnell became defensive.

"It seems," he said on an ABC newscast, "we've acquired a bunch of fleas who are in the business of annoying us." Shanks responded by putting a photo of Strugnell on the cover of the March/April issue of *BAR*. The cover, including the photo, was covered with large fleas.

Yet another well-intended move had unintended results. In 1988, some thirty copies of a concordance to the Scrolls that had been compiled in the 1950s were made and distributed to various academic institutions to facilitate the work of scholars. One of these copies was at Hebrew Union College in Cincinnati. Martin Abegg, who was completing his PhD there under the direction of Ben Zion Wacholder, set about reconstructing the texts from the concordance with the aid of a computer. In September 1991, the first fascicle of reconstructed texts was published by Shanks's *Biblical Archaeology Society*. The ethics of this action was debated in the *New York Times* and *Washington Post*. From the viewpoint of the official editors, it was an act of theft. Shanks responded that the texts rightly belonged to the public. The editorial writers tended to accept the latter argument.

By this time Strugnell's tenure as editor-in-chief was drawing to a close. In October 1990, Emanuel Tov was appointed to serve as co-adjutor editor-in-chief. Eugene Ulrich was appointed co-editor for the biblical scrolls. The critics were not appeased. The Scrolls were still under tight editorial control. In November 1990, however, Strugnell's position became untenable, when an interview he gave to an Israeli journalist, Avi Katzman, was published in the newspaper *Ha'aretz* (November 9, 1990). A modified version was printed in *BAR* in the January/February 1991 issue. In this interview, Strugnell declared himself an "anti-Judaist" and made negative remarks about the Jewish religion. Judaism was "a horrible religion" which should have disappeared through conversion.

Strugnell had always been quaintly old-fashioned in his theology. (He once argued that the ascension of Jesus to heaven was an empirically established fact, because the disciples had seen him depart in an upward direction.) He took a perverse delight in being politically incorrect, whether the subject was the Vietnam war, feminism, or theology. He liked to bait his liberal friends, and they reacted indulgently. No one took him very seriously on these matters. Many Christian scholars were critical of the Israeli takeover of the West Bank. And undoubtedly many Christian theologians remain supersessionist, that is, they think that Judaism has been superseded by Christianity, despite disavowals by Church authorities, although few are so indiscreet as to say so. The statements in the interview, however, went beyond anything that his friends could have anticipated. His manic depression and alcoholism were no doubt contributing factors, and he was goaded on by Katzman. In a later interview with Shanks, in *BAR* July/August 1994, he disavowed responsibility for the formulation of his remarks in the *Ha'aretz* interview, and expressed his position as a belief in the superiority of Christianity rather than a judgment on Judaism. Strugnell had a strong record of helpfulness and collaboration with Jewish students and young scholars, including several Israelis. It was he who first brought Jewish scholars into the editorial team. Eighty-five scholars signed a letter to *BAR* offering a qualified defense, not of the sentiments expressed in the interview, but of the man. "While we find these remarks abhorrent, it is our understanding that they were made at a time when he was seriously ill. We cannot know how much his illness influenced what he said." They remained "deeply grateful to a man who has contributed so much to the study of ancient Judaism." Several of the signatories were Jewish.

Not everyone was so indulgent. One prominent scholar reputedly declared that Strugnell had "drenched the Scrolls in the blood of the Holocaust." Editorial writers at the *New York Times* rushed to the moral high ground. The decision to remove Strugnell from his post as editor-in-chief had apparently been made even before the interview with Katzman. Now it was inevitable. He was replaced by a triumvirate of Emanuel Tov, Eugene Ulrich, and Émile Puech. Eventually, Tov would assume primary responsibility for the publication process. Strugnell was hospitalized on his return to the United States and he was placed on medical leave from Harvard. He would yet make some significant contributions to the edition of major texts (4QMMT, which did not appear until 1994, and a lengthy wisdom text called 4QInstruction). But his career, and his health, were essentially ruined.

It is to the great credit of a number of Jewish and Israeli scholars, including Emanuel Tov, and the young Israeli couple, Hanan and Esther Eshel, that they continued to befriend Strugnell after this debacle, and to show understanding for his condition. He had been kind and helpful to them, and they remained loyal to him. He received strong support from former students and friends who genuinely abhorred the sentiments expressed in the interview. Even Hershel Shanks, who insists with some justification that Strugnell was "an intellectual anti-Semite," came to speak of him as "a Christian gentleman," who continued to meet Shanks and dine with him when the editor came to Cambridge, Massachusetts, even though Shanks had played a major role in ruining his life. Strugnell was a flawed character, to be sure, but he was never malicious. That is more than could be said for some of his most vocal detractors. He died in 2007.

The Huntington Library

The eventual decision to make photographs of the Scrolls available to anyone who wanted to consult them came about through a strange chain of events. Elizabeth Hay Bechtel, a Californian philanthropist, had made significant financial contributions to the publication of the Scrolls. Consequently, in the early 1980s, she obtained two sets of photographic negatives of the Scrolls. One she deposited in the Ancient Biblical Manuscript Center (ABMC) at Claremont, which she had funded. The other, she kept for herself. Subsequently, however, she had a severe falling out with the director of the ABMC, James A. Sanders, and deposited her second copy of the Scrolls in the Huntington Library, a prestigious institution that specialized in Renaissance Literature and in English and American history. In making the donation, Mrs. Bechtel asserted her right of ownership and placed no restrictions on access. This took place in 1982. The Scrolls were remote from the dominant interests of the Library, and they attracted little attention there.

When the triumvirate of Tov, Ulrich, and Puech assumed responsibility for the Scrolls, however, they were concerned that a set of photographs lay beyond their control. In July 1991, Ulrich wrote to William Moffett, who had become librarian of the Huntington in 1990, asking for the return of the set of photos that had been deposited at the Huntington.[2] The request had the opposite effect from what was intended. On September 22, 1991, Moffett announced that the photos of the Scrolls were available to any authorized reader at the Huntington. The announcement was met with protests from the editors and from the Israel Antiquities Authority. Tov wrote to the librarian that he had a legal and moral obligation not to release the photographs. The director of the Israel Antiquities Authority (IAA), Amir Drori, declared that the Huntington's action was "not ethical." The news media, however, sided with the Library. William Safire, in the *New York Times*, called the IAA officials "insular jerks." On October 27, 1991, the IAA dropped its resistance and lifted all restrictions on access to the Scrolls.

The Eisenman-Wise Affair

The lifting of restrictions, however, did not bring an end to all controversy. About a year later, Robert Eisenman and Michael Wise published a book entitled *The Dead Sea Scrolls Uncovered. The First Complete Translation and Interpretation of 50 Key Documents Withheld for Over 35 Years* (Rockport, MA: Element, 1992). Eisenman had become prominent in the campaign for the release of the Scrolls. "As a result," he wrote in the Introduction to the book, "photographs of the remaining unpublished Dead Sea Scrolls were made available to him. These began coming to him in September of 1989. At first they came in small consignments, then more insistently, until by the autumn of 1990, a year later, photographs of virtually the whole of the unpublished corpus and then some, had been made over to him." The source of these photographs has never been disclosed.

Eisenman proceeded to take two actions with this material. On the one hand, he prepared a facsimile edition of all unpublished plates. At first, this was to be published by E. J. Brill of Leiden, but ten days before the scheduled publication in April 1991, Brill withdrew from the project. Hershel Shanks leaped into the breach. In November 1991, the two-volume *Facsimile Edition* was published by the Biblical Archaeology Society. By that time the restrictions on access to the Scrolls had been lifted, but the *Facsimile Edition* made photographs readily available to scholars who did not have easy access to them. It was published under the names of Eisenman and James M. Robinson, a senior New Testament scholar who had played a prominent role in breaking a similar monopoly on the Coptic texts from Nag Hammadi several years earlier, but who never worked on the Scrolls. The Introduction emphasized that this edition was in no way definitive. It consisted of a collection of photographs, without commentary, and the editors claimed neither credit nor responsibility for the way the fragments were grouped in the photos. The bulk of the photographs were said to go back to the early years after discovery, and did not reflect later work by the official editors. Eisenman and Robinson wrote that they were not privy to the source of the photographs, but that they were satisfied that they did not come from their home institutions, California State University at Long Beach, the Institute for Antiquity and Christianity of Claremont Graduate School or the latter's sister institution, the Ancient Biblical Manuscript Center at Claremont. Nor, they added, did they come from the Huntington Library.

Eisenman also set to work on a critical edition of selected texts. Since he himself claimed no competence in epigraphy or work with manuscripts, he enlisted the help of Michael Wise, then an Assistant Professor at the University of Chicago. Wise was a student and protegé of Norman Golb, but

Golb was not directly involved in this project, although Wise apparently consulted him at various points. According to the Introduction to *The Dead Sea Scrolls Uncovered*, "two teams immediately set to work, one under Professor Eisenman at California State University at Long Beach and one under Professor Wise at the University of Chicago. Their aim was to go through everything—every photograph individually—to see what was there, however long it took, leaving nothing to chance and depending on *no one else's work*." Most, if not all, of the transcriptions were completed by Wise's group at the University of Chicago. In fact, some of the texts included in the volume, such as the controversial "Son of God" text, 4Q246, had already been published in part. A Polish scholar Zdzislaw J. Kapera, had published Strugnell and Qimron's reconstruction of the halachic treatise, 4QMMT (see chapter 4) in his journal, *The Qumran Chronicle*, but had desisted from distributing it after he was rebuked at an international conference in Madrid in March 1991. Other texts had been the subject of lectures by scholars to whom they were assigned. The readings and translations in *The Dead Sea Scrolls Uncovered* were somewhat hastily done, and many would be corrected later, but they drew the attention of scholars to several interesting texts that had not been previously discussed.

The book was controversial for several reasons. The Introduction propounded the view of Eisenman, which was not shared by Wise, that the Scrolls provide "a picture of what Christianity actually was in Palestine,"—a violent, militant, messianic movement. (The German translation of the book was entitled *Jesus und die Urchristen*, "Jesus and the Original Christians.") It implied that the texts had been "withheld" because they would undermine the traditional view of Christianity as a peaceful movement, and also the "official" scholarly view that the texts should be ascribed to the Essenes. The most controversial aspect, however, concerned the ethics of publishing these texts at all without the permission of the editors to whom they had been assigned. More specifically, several scholars charged that Wise and Eisenman had made use of the work of those editors, which they had available in the form of hand-outs or, in the case of 4QMMT, of a pirated edition, and, in effect, had plagiarized them.

The Wise-Eisenman volume appeared a few weeks before a major international conference in New York, sponsored by the New York Academy of Sciences and the Oriental Institute of the University of Chicago, and held at the Blood Center. This conference had been organized by Norman Golb with the assistance of Michael Wise and others.[3] The schedule called for a panel discussion on the ethics of publishing scholarly texts. Golb had envisioned that this panel would roundly condemn the "hoarding" of the Scrolls by the official editorial team prior to 1991. Now, however, the Wise-Eisenman book became the center of discussion. A group of nineteen scholars, including members of the official editorial team, published a letter in the newspapers denouncing the new book. Some prominent scholars, including Tov and Ulrich, refused to attend the conference. In the ethics panel discussion, Lawrence Schiffman delivered a blistering critique of Wise and Eisenman. He insisted that his criticism did not stem from the fact that they had published texts that were assigned to others. Rather, the central point of criticism was that "credit is not sufficiently given to all of the scholars whose work was used in preparing the volume."[4] In several cases, he charged, "the authors depended on handouts distributed at conferences, the existence of which they appear to hide from the readers in order to portray themselves as producing the *editio princeps* of the text in question." He cited three examples, most significantly MMT, where the authors misread John Strugnell's handwriting in one case. Norman Golb responded to "this intemperate attack" on Wise and Eisenman, and questioned the motives of the critics: "While claiming that they are in no way opposed to the publication of Qumran texts by others, the signers of the document . . . attempt to discourage precisely such publication by those whose views on Qumran origins differ radically from their own."[5] He offered his personal attestation of the fact that Wise and the graduate students under his direction had studied the photographs independently. (Schiffman had not denied that they had done original work, but claimed that they had also used the work of other scholars without fully acknowledging it.) Wise pointed out that the new edition of 4QMMT differed from the Strugnell-Qimron edition at dozens of points, and actually regarded it as two texts. He also noted that the subtitle of the book ("documents withheld for over 35 years") had been imposed by the publisher. Heated discussion followed. (The irony of the name of the building, the Blood Center, did not go unnoticed.) After the panel, a few scholars met with Wise with a view to resolving the conflict. At the end of the conference, Wise issued a statement that he had come to understand the position of his critics more fully. "I regret the impression, unintended by me, which emerges from the introduction concerning the degree to which some parts of the work were done independently. I am sorry that the documentation for certain portions of the book for which I was responsible was incomplete, and that I did not more fully express indebtedness to colleagues whose work I consulted ... It is more-over regrettable that I did not have adequate input into the final form of the book, and that is some-thing that should not have happened."[6] In response, the scholars who had signed the public statement of condemnation retracted it.

Since fuller editions of many of the texts in ques-tion appeared in the next few years (several by Émile Puech), the importance of the Wise-Eisenman vol-ume was short-lived. Nonetheless, it contains some interesting readings, and is still worth consulting. Some scholars, notably Puech, continue to regard it as a work of plagiarism and refuse to cite it. Wise was denied tenure at the University of Chicago, but he has subsequently written several important stud-ies on the Dead Sea Scrolls.[7]

The Qimron-Shanks Lawsuit

When Zdzislaw Kapera published the composite text of 4QMMT, he had been threatened with a lawsuit by the Israel Antiquities Authority. He apol-ogized, and refrained from further distribution. When Hershel Shanks published the same text in his Publisher's Foreword to the *Facsimile Edition of the Dead Sea Scrolls*, edited by Eisenman and Rob-inson, however, Elisha Qimron sued in an Israeli court. Shanks, in his Foreword, had acknowledged that the transcription was the work of Strugnell, and that the commentary was his work "with a colleague," but he did not mention Qimron's name. He later claimed that the reason for the omission was that he did not want to appear harshly critical of a young, untenured, scholar, but he admits that practically no one believes this.[8] Eisenman and Robinson were included in the lawsuit, but Shanks had accepted primary responsibility.

The Israeli court asserted its right to try the case, on the grounds that three copies of the book had been mailed to Israel. It promptly issued an injunction prohibiting the defendants from distributing the reconstructed text. Consequently, it was omitted from the second edition of the *Facsimile Edition*. The trial took place in February 1993. The court found in Qimron's favor, and awarded him a total of 100,000 New Israeli Shekels (more than $40,000) as compensation for loss of earnings and mental distress. (He had requested between three and four times that amount.) Shanks appealed, but the Israeli Supreme Court upheld the decision. Since Shanks had to pay Qimron's lawyer's fees as well as his own, in both courts, the trial cost him in excess of $100,000.

The lawsuit was remarkable in several respects. An ancient text cannot be claimed as personal property by a modern scholar. The merits of this case rested on the extent of Qimron's creativity in reconstructing the text. If it could be shown that the reconstruction was entirely accurate, it would not be protected by copyright. But in fact, while Qimron played an important role in the *interpretation* of the text, he seems to have played only a very minor role in reconstructing it. The photographic record of the Scrolls shows that the text had been substantially reconstructed by 1961, long before Qimron came on the scene. Qimron only cited two cases where he had made relatively minor adjustments. Accordingly, it would seem that the main credit for reconstructing this scroll should go to John Strugnell, who did not join the lawsuit. When this was pointed out in a review by Florentino García Martínez, a highly respected authority on the Scrolls, who taught at the University of Groningen in the Netherlands and the University of Leuven, in Belgium, Qimron demanded an apology for defamation of character and threatened to utilize "all legitimate means at his disposal to redress this wrong," but he subsequently dropped the matter. Nonetheless, the official edition of 4QMMT in *Discoveries in the Judean Desert*, volume 10, which appeared in 1994, was copyrighted in Qimron's name alone, without derogating from the rights of the Israel Antiquities Authority.

The judgment of the Israeli court has been widely discussed, and legal opinions are sharply divided about it.[9] It seems unlikely that an American court would have reached the same decision. Most scholars can attest that the potential financial income from editing a volume or from lecturing on the Dead Sea Scrolls seldom reaches the amount awarded to Qimron, much less the amount he claimed. It might well be argued that his reputation for litigiousness has hurt his subsequent career far more than Shanks's unauthorized publication of MMT, which could be viewed as free publicity.

The irrepressible Shanks still tweaked Qimron's nose one more time. After the official publication of 4QMMT in 1994, Shanks requested and obtained permission from Oxford University Press to reproduce the text and translation in the *Biblical Archaeology Review*. Qimron threatened to have him held in contempt of court, and prevailed on Oxford University Press to send Shanks a letter, protesting that his request for permission to republish the text had been disingenuous. In this case, too, Qimron eventually decided to let the matter lapse.

Rafael Golb

There would be yet another lawsuit relating to the Dead Sea Scrolls, arguably the most bizarre of all.

On November 19, 2010, the *New York Times* reported on page A24 that Rafael Golb, son of Norman Golb, was convicted in the State Supreme Court in Manhattan of establishing e-mail accounts pretending to be Lawrence Schiffman, and sending messages to university officials in which Schiffman supposedly confessed to plagiarism. Golb, a fifty-year-old real estate lawyer in New York, with a PhD from Harvard, said that the e-mails were merely parodies, but that he believed that Schiffman had plagiarized the work of his father Norman. (Schiffman and the elder Golb disagree on most issues relating to the Scrolls.) Golb had allegedly also sent e-mails in the name of other scholars, and sometimes anonymous e-mails, complaining that exhibitions of the Scrolls did not adequately represent the views of his father. (The father has been consistently and vocally critical of museum exhibits on the Scrolls, in blogs and letters to board members.) The younger Golb was present at the conference in the Blood Center in New York in 1992, when Schiffman had taken the lead in criticizing the work of Wise and Eisenman. His motivation has not been articulated, but it would seem to arise from a concern to defend his father's views and to discomfit his perceived opponents. At the time of writing he has appealed his conviction.

Why the Fury?

Two famous sayings come to mind in rehearsing these disputes. One is Henry Kissinger's dictum that academic disputes are so bitter because there is so little at stake. The other is Edmund Burke's judgment on the French revolution: "vanity made the revolution; liberty was only the excuse."

There can be little doubt that scholarly, and unscholarly, egos played an enormous role in the most heated disputes. Editors who were reluctant to make texts available to other scholars were guarding their position of privilege, even if they honestly believed that open access would lead to the proliferation of nonsense by incompetent headline seekers. Those who pressed most vocally for the release of the scrolls were not free of self-interest, either. There were reputations to be made and standing in the scholarly world to be achieved. Scholars set great store by claims to have been the first to publish something, even though the significance of the achievement may not be universally appreciated. Heated debates sometimes gave rise to personal animosities, and these contributed to some of the most bitter controversies. It should be said, however, that the acrimonious disputes involved only a small number of people at any time. Most scholars in the field have good collegial relations and only a limited appetite for controversy.

That said, the release of the Scrolls was unequivocally a good thing. Despite the dire warnings of the official editors, chaos did not result. There has been wild speculation on occasion, to be sure, but the marketplace of ideas has a way of eventually separating the wheat from the chaff. The whole episode can serve as a lesson for the way future discoveries should be handled. The privileges of editors to whom material is assigned cannot be extended indefinitely. Scholarship is best served by making material available promptly in provisional form rather than waiting for supposedly definitive editions that might take a lifetime to produce.

The reason why the Scrolls, more than other notable discoveries such as the Coptic codices from Nag Hammadi in Egypt, caught the imagination of the public is due to the fact that they come from a time and place of exceptional importance in the history of the Western world. As primary documents from Judea in the time of Jesus, they offer a window on the context in which Christianity was born, if not directly on the movement itself. More directly, they give us an unprecedented view of what Judaism was like before the destruction of Jerusalem and the rise of the rabbinic movement. Like all archeological discoveries, they provide raw data, unedited by later authorities, and consequently offer the hope of insight into how things really were before the church and the synagogue constructed their official genealogies. The stakes, then, for both Judaism and Christianity are considerable, since the new discoveries potentially place official accounts in question and undercut the authority of religious authorities.

Several attempts have been made to exploit that potential and to use the Scrolls as evidence against the veracity of traditional Christianity, and to a lesser extent, of traditional Judaism. The most widely known of these attempts is that of the English writers Michael Baigent and Richard Leigh, in their 1991 book, *The Dead Sea Scrolls Deception*, who darkly hinted at a Vatican conspiracy to suppress the truth. They accepted the view of Robert Eisenman, that the Scrolls represent messianic Judaism, including the Jesus movement, in the first century CE, and that this movement was vastly different from the way it is portrayed in the Gospels. Far from being peace-loving, it was xenophobic and militant. Eisenman's views were also endorsed by another popular writer on subjects relating to Near Eastern Archeology, Neil Asher Silberman, in his 1994 book, *The Hidden Scrolls*. Neither Baigent and Leigh nor Silberman were scholars trained in this material, and their judgment was utterly at variance with that of the scholarly community. Scarcely any scholar has found Eisenman's reading of the Scrolls persuasive at all. (Neither does any reputable scholar give any credence to the rumored "Vatican conspiracy.") But Eisenman's work has garnered attention, because it is a dramatic representation of the kind of conflict between received tradition and new discovery that for many people is the lure of archeology. If he were proved right, it would show that the great religious traditions of Judaism and Christianity were built on misrepresentations of their origins. This possibility was obviously appealing to writers who sought to attract public attention. No one sells books by showing that what we believed all along turns out to be true.

But for better or worse, the Scrolls do not overturn either Judaism or Christianity in this dramatic fashion. They show that some ideas of early Christianity (e.g., that the messiah could be regarded as son of God) were not unprecedented. Some scholars have been a shade defensive about this, but in fact scholars have always known that the early Christians adapted Jewish and other ideas in various ways. Of course the Scrolls do not confirm any particular set of religious beliefs either. They show that certain forms of Judaism were already well attested in the first century BCE, and that the traditional text of the Hebrew Bible goes back to pre-Christian times, even if other forms of the text were also known around the turn of the era. The fundamental claims of divine revelation on which both Judaism and Christianity are based, however, are not so easily confirmed or disconfirmed by any historical discovery.

The Scrolls are not great literature, with the arguable exception of the religious poetry of the *Hodayot* or Thanksgiving Hymns, and, of course, of the biblical texts. Neither do they contain any great new religious insights that might transform modern theology. The core of the corpus is made up of sectarian writings. While these writings are not as xenophobic or hate-filled as Eisenman and his followers would have it, they reflect the views of religious extremists, who tried to separate themselves from the world. There is a reason why this movement did not survive, and why its tenets were not taken up by mainline Judaism. They were simply too extreme to have enduring appeal.

Nonetheless, the Scrolls are of extraordinary historical importance. Before their discovery, we had no literature in Hebrew or Aramaic from Judea in the period between the Maccabees and the Mishnah. The Scrolls fill out our knowledge of Judaism in this period in countless ways. Despite the sectarian ideology of much of the corpus, it also includes much material that is reflective of the common Judaism of the time. Much of the debate about the

Essene hypothesis has been fueled by conflicting desires to see the Scrolls as marginal and negligible, on the one hand, or as representative of mainline Judaism on the other. Neither of these categorizations can be sustained in isolation. The sectarian movement reflected in the Scrolls was marginal, insofar as it was a movement that died out and had no discernible influence on later Jewish tradition. But it was not completely isolated, and the writings found in the caves are illuminating in many ways for the Judaism of the time.

As scholars have increasingly recognized in the last quarter century, the Scrolls are documents of ancient Judaism. Despite sensationalist claims, they are not Christian, and do not witness directly to Jesus of Nazareth and his followers. Nonetheless, they illuminate the context in which Jesus lived, and in which earliest Christianity took shape. While the Scrolls sometimes provide parallels to particular ideas in the New Testament, more often they provide a foil. The ways of the Teacher of Righteousness and of Jesus were alternative paths in the context of ancient Judaism, different ways in which the Jewish tradition might be appropriated and different interpretations of its scriptures.

All the Scrolls have now finally been delivered to the light of day. The biography of the corpus is still in its adolescence. Its early years have been turbulent, but we may hope that it will benefit from mature scholarship in the years ahead.

Further Reading

Informative accounts of "the battle to free the Scrolls," with due attention to the role played by the authors, can be found in Hershel Shanks, *Freeing the Dead Sea Scrolls and Other Adventures of an Archaeology Outsider* (New York: Continuum, 2010) and Geza Vermes, *The Story of the Scrolls. The Miraculous Discovery and True Significance of the Dead Sea Scrolls* (London: Penguin, 2010). The account by Neil Asher Silberman, *The Hidden Scrolls. Christianity, Judaism and the War for the Dead Sea Scrolls* (New York: Putnam, 1994), is flawed by his uncritical acceptance of the viewpoint of Robert Eisenman and by his lack of mastery of the scholarship on the Scrolls.

The debate over the Eisenman-Wise book, *The Dead Sea Scrolls Uncovered*, is recorded in M. O. Wise, N. Golb, J. J. Collins, and D. G. Pardee, eds., *Methods of Investigation of the Dead Sea Scrolls and the Khirbet Qumran Site. Present Realities and Future Prospects* (New York: New York Academy of Sciences, 1994), 455–97.

The book of Michael Baigent and Richard Leigh, *The Dead Sea Scrolls Deception* (London: Jonathan Cape, 1991), is engagingly written but is now something of an historical curiosity.

An objective account of the controversies over the Scrolls, insofar as such a thing is possible, can found in James VanderKam and Peter Flint, *The Meaning of the Dead Sea Scrolls. Their Significance for Understanding the Bible, Judaism, Jesus, and Christianity* (San Francisco: HarperSanFrancisco, 2002), 381–403.

Personalities in the Discovery and Subsequent Controversies

APPENDIX

Albright, William Foxwell: Dominant figure in scholarship on Bible and Ancient Near East in the mid-twentieth century. Verified the antiquity of the Dead Sea Scrolls on the basis of paleography.

Allegro, John Marco: Maverick member of the editorial team who suggested that the Scrolls anticipated key elements of Christianity.

Baigent, Michael and Richard Leigh: Sensationalist British authors who alleged a Vatican cover-up of the significance of the Scrolls.

Brownlee, William H.: Fellow at the American Schools when the first Scrolls were brought there. Later professor at Claremont.

Burrows, Millar: Yale professor. Director of American Schools in Jerusalem in 1948. Author of first press release on the Scrolls, and later of influential accounts of the corpus.

Cross, Frank Moore: Key figure in editorial team. Expert in paleography and text criticism. Author of very influential account of the Scrolls, *The Ancient Library of Qumran*. Later long-time professor at Harvard.

Dupont-Sommer, André: French professor. Early champion of Essene hypothesis. Believed that the Essenes anticipated Christianity in many ways.

Eisenman, Robert: Controversial figure in "the battle for the Scrolls." Argued that the Scrolls were authentic documents of the early Christian movement.

Golb, Norman: Long-time professor at University of Chicago. Vehement critic of Essene hypothesis. Claims Scrolls came from Jerusalem. His son Rafael was convicted of impersonating a rival scholar to discredit him.

Kando, Khalil Iskander Shahin: Cobbler in Bethlehem who became a major middle-man between the Bedouin and people interested in acquiring the Scrolls.

Knohl, Israel: Israeli scholar who claimed to find a "messiah before Jesus," who was also raised from the dead and exalted to heaven, in the Scrolls.

Kuhn, Karl-Georg: Ex-Nazi, who became an influential Scrolls scholar. Championed Zoroastrian background of dualism in the Scrolls.

Magness, Jodi: Major authority on archeology of Qumran in late twentieth and early twenty-first centuries.

Milik, Józef T.: Polish priest. Member of editorial team. Brilliant at deciphering ancient texts. Later left priesthood.

Mohammed ed-Dib: Bedouin credited with initial
discovery of Dead Sea Scrolls.

Puech, Émile: French priest who was major figure in
publication of Scrolls after 1991. Member of triumvirate appointed to succeed Strugnell in 1990.

Qimron, Elisha: Israeli scholar. Co-editor of 4QMMT.
Later involved in litigation over copyright.

Renan, Ernst: French intellectual in nineteenth century, who said that Christianity was an Essenism
that survived.

Samuel, Mar Athanasius: Syrian archbishop in Jerusalem, who obtained some Scrolls and advertised
them for sale in the *Wall Street Journal.*

Schiffman, Lawrence: Influential advocate of the Jewish character of the Scrolls.

Shanks, Hershel: Editor of *Biblical Archeology Review.*
Tireless campaigner for release of the Scrolls. Later
sued by Qimron for breach of copyright.

Strugnell, John: Youngest member of the editorial
team. Editor-in-chief 1985–90. Forced to resign in
controversial circumstances.

Sukenik, Eliezer Lippa: First Israeli scholar to examine
and validate the Scrolls. Author of some of the earliest surveys. Early advocate of the Essene hypothesis.

Tov, Emanuel: Israeli text-critical scholar who oversaw
the publication of the Scrolls from 1991 on.

Trever, John C.: Fellow at American Schools when
Scrolls were discovered. Took first photographs of
Scrolls.

Ulrich, Eugene C.: Text-critical scholar. Member of triumvirate appointed to succeed Strugnell in 1990.

De Vaux, Roland, O.P.: French Dominican priest at École Biblique in Jerusalem. Excavator of Qumran. Supervised publication of Scrolls until his death in 1971.

Vermes, Geza: Long-time Oxford professor. Excluded from editorial team until 1990s. Author of standard translation of the Scrolls.

Wilson, Edmund: American journalist who fanned controversy over the relation of the Scrolls to Christianity in 1950s.

Wise, Michael O.: Co-editor, with Robert Eisenman, of controversial edition of unpublished Dead Sea Scrolls in 1992. Later authored controversial study of the Teacher of Righteousness as "the first messiah."

Yadin, Yigael: Son of Sukenik. Archeologist, scholar, soldier, statesman. Acquired for Israel Scrolls offered for sale by Syrian Archbishop. Later acquired Temple Scroll from Kando after 1967 war.

CHAPTER 1: The Discovery of the Scrolls

1. Frank Moore Cross, *The Ancient Library of Qumran and Modern Biblical Studies* (3rd ed.; Sheffield: Sheffield Academic Press, 1995, originally published by Doubleday in 1958), 38.

2. Cross, *The Ancient Library of Qumran.* Compare the title of the English translation of Hartmut Stegemann's book, *Die Essener, Qumran, Johannes der Täufer und Jesus* (Freiburg im Breisgau: Herder, 1993): *The Library of Qumran. On the Essenes, Qumran, John the Baptist, and Jesus* (Grand Rapids, MI: Eerdmans, 1998).

3. Stegemann, *The Library of Qumran*, 84.

4. Emanuel Tov, *Scribal Practices and Approaches Reflected in the Texts Found in the Judean Desert* (STDJ 54; Leiden: Brill, 2004), 261–88.

5. K.-H. Rengstorff, *Hirbet Qumran and the Problem of the Dead Sea Cave Scrolls* (Leiden: Brill, 1963).

6. K. G. Kuhn, "Les rouleaux de cuivre de Qumrân," *Revue Biblique* 61(1954): 193–205.

7. J. T. Milik, *Ten Years of Discovery in the Wilderness of Judaea* (Studies in Biblical Theology 26; London: SCM, 1959), 42–43. For de Vaux's alleged remark, see Norman Golb, *Who Wrote the Dead Sea Scrolls? The Search for the Secret of Qumran* (New York: Scribner, 1995), 121.

CHAPTER 2: The Essenes

1. Weston W. Fields, *The Dead Sea Scrolls. A Full History* (Leiden: Brill, 2009), 58.
2. Fields, *The Dead Sea Scrolls*, 87.
3. Neil Asher Silberman, "Sukenik, Eleazar L.," in Lawrence H. Schiffman and James C. VanderKam, eds., *The Encyclopedia of the Dead Sea Scrolls* (New York: Oxford, 2000), 903.
4. Robert Taylor, *The Diegesis, Being a Discovery of the Origin, Evidences, and Early History of Christianity* (Boston: Kneeland, 1834), 38.
5. Isaak M. Jost, *Geschichte des Judenthums und seiner Secten, vol. 1* (Leipzig, 1857), 207–15, quoted as translated by Christian D. Ginsburg, *The Essenes. Their History and Doctrines* (London: Routledge & Kegan Paul, 1955), 78.
6. Emil Schuerer, *Geschichte des Jüdischen Volkes im Zeitalter Jesu Christi* (3rd ed.; Leipzig: Hinrichs, 1898), 2.577.
7. I. Lévy, *La Légende de Pythagore de Grèce en Palestine* (Paris: Champion, 1927), 289.
8. J. B. Lightfoot, *Saint Paul's Epistles to the Colossians and to Philemon* (11th ed.; London and New York, 1892), 80–96, 347–417.

9. M. Friedländer, "Les Esséniens," *Revue des Études Juives* 14 (1887): 184–216.

10. Louis Ginzberg, *An Unknown Jewish Sect* (New York: Jewish Theological Seminary, 1970; originally published privately by the author as *Eine unbekannte jüdische Sekte* (New York, 1922).

11. Roland de Vaux, *Archaeology and the Dead Sea Scrolls* (London: Oxford University Press for the British Academy, 1973), 133.

12. Chaim Rabin, *Qumran Studies* (Oxford: Oxford University Press, 1957), 69.

13. G. R. Driver, *The Judaean Scrolls. The Problem and a Solution* (Oxford: Blackwell, 1965); Cecil Roth, *The Historical Background of the Dead Sea Scrolls* (New York: Philosophical Library, 1959).

14. Barbara Thiering, *Jesus and the Riddle of the Dead Sea Scrolls: Unlocking the Secrets of His Life Story* (San Francisco: Harper Collins, 1992).

15. Robert Eisenman in R. H. Eisenman and M. O. Wise, eds., *The Dead Sea Scrolls Uncovered. The First Complete Translation and Interpretation of 50 Key Documents Withheld for Over 35 Years* (Rockport, MA: Element, 1992), 10. See also Eisenman, *Maccabees, Zadokites, Christians and Qumran: A New Hypothesis of Qumran Origins* (Leiden: Brill, 1983); Eisenman, *James The Brother of Jesus: The Key to Unlocking the Secrets of Early Christianity and the Dead Sea Scrolls* (New York: Viking, 1997).

16. Saul Lieberman, "Discipline in the So-Called Dead Sea Manual of Discipline," *Journal of Biblical Literature* 73 (1952): 199–206.

17. Frank Moore Cross, "The Early History of the Qumran Community," in David Noel Freedman and Jonas C. Greenfield, *New Directions in Biblical Archaeology* (Garden City, NY: Doubleday, 1969), 68–69.

CHAPTER 3: The Site of Qumran

1. Roland de Vaux, *Archaeology and the Dead Sea Scrolls* (London: Oxford University Press, 1973).

2. Jean-Baptiste Humbert and Alain Chambon, *Fouilles de Khirbet Qumrân et de ʿAin Feshkha: Album de photographies, Répertoire du fonds photographique, Synthèse des notes de chantier du Père Roland de Vaux OP* (Fribourg: Éditions Universitaires, 1994); Stephen J. Pfann, *The Excavations of Khirbet Qumran and ʿAin Feshkha: Synthesis of Roland de Vaux's Field Notes* (Fribourg: University Press, 2003).

3. Magen Broshi and Hanan Eshel, "How and Where Did the Qumranites Live?" in Donald W. Parry and Eugene Ulrich, eds., *The Provo International Conference on the Dead Sea Scrolls* (STDJ 30; Leiden: Brill, 1999), 266–73.

4. Jodi Magness, *The Archaeology of Qumran and the Dead Sea Scrolls* (Grand Rapids, MI: Eerdmans, 2002), 65.

5. De Vaux, *Archaeology*, 111–12.

6. Magness, *The Archaeology of Qumran*, 175.

7. Cross, *The Ancient Library*, 70 (1961 edition).

8. Adolfo Roitman, ed., *A Day at Qumran. The Dead Sea Sect and its Scrolls* (Jerusalem: The Israel Museum, 1997).

9. Pauline Donceel-Voûte, "Les ruines de Qumrân reinterprétées," *Archaeologia* 298 (1994): 28–35; Robert Donceel and Pauline Donceel-Voûte, "The Archaeology of Khirbet Qumran," in Michael O. Wise, Norman Golb, John J. Collins, and Dennis G. Pardee, eds., *Methods of Investigation of the Dead Sea Scrolls and the Khirbet Qumran Site: Present Realities and Future Prospects* (New York: New York Academy of Sciences, 1994), 1–38.

10. Y. Hirschfeld, *Qumran in Context* (Peabody, MA: Hendrickson, 2004), 142.

11. J. B. Humbert, "Reconsideration of the Archaeological Interpretation," in Jean-Baptiste Humbert and Jan Gunneweg, eds., *Khirbet Qumrân et ʿAïn Feshkha II: Études d'anthropologie, de physique et de chimie. Studies of Anthropology, Physics and Chemistry* (Fribourg: Academic Press, 2003), 422.

12. Magness, *The Archaeology of Qumran*, 90–100; "A Villa at Khirbet Qumran?" in Magness, *Debating Qumran: Collected Essays on Archaeology* (Leuven: Peeters, 2004), 17–39.

13. Alan D. Crown and Lena Cansdale, "Qumran—Was it an Essene Settlement?" *Biblical Archaeological Review* 20 (1994): 24–37, 73–78.

14. Yizhak Magen and Yuval Peleg, "Back to Qumran: Ten Years of Excavation and Research, 1993 to 2004," in Katharina Galor, Jean-Baptiste Humbert, and Jürgen Zangenberg, eds., *Qumran: The Site of the Dead Sea Scrolls: Archaeological Interpretations and Debates. Proceedings of a Conference Held at Brown University, November 17–19, 2002* (STDJ 57; Leiden: Brill, 2006), 55–113.

15. De Vaux, *Archaeology*, 42.

16. This point was argued especially by Norman Golb, *Who Wrote the Dead Sea Scrolls?* 39–40.

17. Robert Cargill, *Qumran Through Real Time. A Virtual Reconstruction of Qumran and the Dead Sea Scrolls* (Piscataway, NJ: Gorgias, 2009).

18. Golb, *Who Wrote the Dead Sea Scrolls*, 34.

19. Yitzhar Hirschfeld, "A Settlement of Hermits above ʿEn Gedi," *Tel Aviv* 27 (2000): 1–35; David Amit and Jodi Magness, "Not a Settlement of Hermits. A Response to Y. Hirschfeld, "A Settlement of Hermits above ʿEn Gedi," *Tel Aviv* 27 (2000): 273–85.

CHAPTER 4: The Scrolls and Christianity

1. See Robert Eisenman in R. H. Eisenman and M. O. Wise, eds., *The Dead Sea Scrolls Uncovered. The First Complete Translation and Interpretation of 50 Key Documents Withheld for Over 35 Years* (Rockport, MA: Element, 1992), 10.

2. A. Dupont-Sommer, *Observations sur le Commentaire d'Habacuc découvert près de la Mer Morte* (Paris: Adrien-Maisonneuve, 1950), 29, trans. Geza Vermes, *The Story of the Scrolls. The Miraculous Discovery and True Significance of the Dead Sea Scrolls* (London: Penguin, 2010), 59. The lecture was reported in *Le Monde*, May 28–29, 1950, p. 4.

3. A. Dupont-Sommer, *The Dead Sea Scrolls: a Preliminary Survey* (Oxford: Blackwell, 1952), 99–100, translated from his *Aperçus preliminaries sur les manuscripts de la mer Morte* (Paris: Maisonneuve, 1950).

4. Dupont-Sommer, *The Essene Writings from Qumran* (trans. G. Vermes; Gloucester, MA: Smith, 1973), 361.

5. Wilson, *The Dead Sea Scrolls, 1947–1969* (New York: Oxford, 1969), 4–748.

6. Wilson, *The Dead Sea Scrolls*, 98.

7. Wilson, *The Dead Sea Scrolls*, 99.

8. Allegro's radio broadcast, as cited by Michael Baigent and Richard Leigh, *The Dead Sea Scrolls Deception* (London: Jonathan Cape, 1991), 46.

9. Allegro's radio broadcast, cited from Judith Anne Brown, *John Marco Allegro, The Maverick of the Dead Sea Scrolls* (Grand Rapids, MI: Eerdmans, 2005), 77.

10. *The Times*, March 26, 1956, p. 11.

11. Quoted from Fields, *The Dead Sea Scrolls. A Full History*, 310.

12. Brown, *John Marco Allegro*, 185.

13. Baigent and Leigh, *The Dead Sea Scrolls Deception*, 56.

14. D. Barthélemy, O.P. and J. T. Milik, *Qumran Cave 1* (DJD 1; Oxford: Clarendon, 1955), 108–17.

15. Joseph A. Fitzmyer, "The Contribution of Qumran Aramaic to the Study of the New Testament," *NTS* 20 (1973–74): 382–407.

16. É. Puech, "Fragment d'une apocalypse en Aramée (4Q246=ps Dan^d) et le 'Royaume de Dieu,'" *Revue Biblique* 99 (1992): 98–131.

17. Joseph A. Fitzmyer, *The One Who Is To Come* (Grand Rapids, MI: Eerdmans, 2007), 106–7.

18. Joseph A. Fitzmyer, *The Gospel According to Luke I–IX* (AB 28; New York: Doubleday, 1981), 207.

19. Israel Knohl, *The Messiah before Jesus* (Berkeley: University of California Press, 2000), 42.

20. J. A. Fitzmyer, *Responses to 101 Questions on the Dead Sea Scrolls* (Mahwah, NJ: Paulist, 1992), 106.

21. J. H. Charlesworth, "John the Baptizer and the Dead Sea Scrolls," in idem, ed., *The Bible and the Dead Sea Scrolls* (Waco: Baylor, 2006), 1–35 (quotation from p. 34).

22. Millar Burrows, *The Dead Sea Scrolls* (New York: Viking, 1955), 329.

23. Cross, *The Ancient Library of Qumran* (3rd ed.; Sheffield: Sheffield Academic Press, 1995), 144.

24. Cross, *The Ancient Library of Qumran*, 145.

25. R. E. Brown, "The Qumran Scrolls and the Johannine Gospel and Epistles," *Catholic Biblical Quarterly* 17(1955): 403–19; 559–74.

26. Cross, *The Ancient Library of Qumran*, 155.

27. Cross, *The Ancient Library of Qumran*, 156.

28. Eisenman, in *The Dead Sea Scrolls Uncovered* (Rockport, MA: Element, 1992), 10.

29. Eisenman, in *The Dead Sea Scrolls Uncovered*.

30. Barbara E. Thiering, *Jesus the Man: New Interpretation from the Dead Sea Scrolls*, reissued in paperback with foreword by Barbara Thiering (New York: Simon & Schuster, 2006).

CHAPTER 5: The Scrolls and Judaism

1. The name comes from Citium in Cyprus, and referred to anyone who came from the west. In 1 Maccabees, Alexander the Great is called king of the Kittim.

2. Dupont-Sommer, *The Dead Sea Scrolls*, 94.

3. Plutarch, *On Isis and Osiris* 47, trans. J. Gwyn Griffiths, *Plutarch's De Iside et Osiride* (Cardiff: University of Wales, 1970), 46–47.

4. K. G. Kuhn, "Die Sektenschrift (1QS) und die iranische Religion," *Zeitschrift für Theologie und Kirche* 49 (1952): 296–316. On Kuhn's career, see Gerhard Lindemann, "Theological Research about Judaism in Different Political Contexts: The Example of Karl Georg Kuhn," *Kirchliche Zeitgeschichte* 17 (2004): 339–51, and, most recently, Gert Jeremias, "Karl Georg Kuhn (1906–1976)," in Cilliers Breytenbach and Rudolf Hoppe, eds., *Neutestamentliche Wissenschaft nach 1945. Hauptvertreter der deutschsprachigen Exegese in der Darstellung ihrer Schüler* (Neukirchen-Vluyn: Neukirchener, 2008), 297–312. Also Gerd Theissen, *Neutestamentliche Wissenschaft vor und nach 1945: Karl Georg Kuhn und Günther Bornkamm* (Schriften der Philosophisch-historischen Klasse der Heidelberger Akademie der Wissenschaften 47; Heidelberg: Universitätsverlag Winter, 2009), 15–149. See also Jörg Frey, "Qumran Research and Biblical Scholarship in Germany," in Dimant, ed., *The Dead Sea Scrolls in Scholarly Perspective*, 529–64, especially 541–6.

5. K. G. Kuhn, "Die in Palästina gefundenen hebräischen Texte," *Zeitschrift für Theologie und Kirche* 47 (1950): 197.

6. Cross, *The Ancient Library of Qumran*, 144.

7. S. Leiberman, "The Discipline in the So-Called Dead Sea Manual of Discipline," *Journal of Biblical Literature* 72 (1952): 199–206.

8. Lieberman, "Light on the Cave Scrolls from Rabbinic Sources," *Proceedings of the American Academy for Jewish Research* 20 (1951): 395–404.

9. C. Rabin, *Qumran Studies* (Oxford: Oxford University Press, 1957), 69.

10. In W. H. Propp, B. Halpern, and D. N. Freedman, eds., *The Hebrew Bible and Its Interpreters* (Winona Lake, IN: Eisenbrauns, 1990), 167–87.

11. Philadelphia and Jerusalem: The Jewish Publication Society, 1994.

CHAPTER 6: The Scrolls and the Bible

1. W. F. Albright, "New Light on Early Recensions of the Hebrew Bible," *BASOR* 140(1955): 27–33.

2. Cross, *The Ancient Library of Qumran*, 138–42.

3. Emanuel Tov, "Groups of Biblical Texts Found at Qumran," in D. Dimant and L. H. Schiffman, eds., *Time to Prepare the Way in the Wilderness: Papers on the Qumran Scrolls* (STDJ 16; Leiden: Brill, 1995), 85–102.

4. Emanuel Tov, ed., *The Texts from the Judaean Desert. Indices and an Introduction to the Discoveries in the Judaean Desert Series* (DJD 39: Oxford: Clarendon, 2002).

5. B. Webster, "Chronological Index to the Texts from the Judaean Desert," in Tov, ed., *The Texts from the Judaean Desert*, 371–75.

6. Emanuel Tov and Sidnie White, "Reworked Pentateuch," *DJD* 13: 187–351.

7. 4QMMT, composite text C 10. The text is reconstructed and sometimes disputed, but is almost certainly correct.

8. J. A. Sanders, *The Psalms Scroll of Qumran Cave 11* (DJD 4; Oxford: Clarendon, 1965).

CHAPTER 7: The Battle for the Scrolls

1. Geza Vermes, *The Dead Sea Scrolls: Qumran in Perspective* (London: Collins, 1977), 23–24.

2. So Hershel Shanks, *Freeing the Dead Sea Scrolls and Other Adventures of an Archaeology Outsider* (New York: Continuum, 2010), 158.

3. The author of this volume was marginally involved. Preparations were well under way when I moved to the University of Chicago in 1991. I was credited as a co-editor of the proceedings, but the work was done by Michael Wise.

4. Schiffman's remarks, and the ensuing discussion, are printed in M. O. Wise, N. Golb, J. J. Collins, and D. G. Pardee, eds., *Methods of Investigation of the Dead Sea Scrolls and the Khirbet Qumran Site. Present Realities and Future Prospects* (New York: New York Academy of Sciences, 1994), 463–68.

5. Wise et al., *Methods of Investigation of the Dead Sea Scrolls*, 473.

6. Wise et al., *Methods of Investigation of the Dead Sea Scrolls*, 496.

7. Notably his book, *The First Messiah. Investigating the Savior before Christ* (San Francisco: HarperSanFrancisco, 1999) and his article "The Origins and History of the Teacher's Movement," in Lim and Collins, eds., *The Oxford Handbook of the Dead Sea Scrolls*, 92–122. He also co-authored a translation of the Scrolls with Martin Abegg and Edward Cook: *The Dead Sea Scrolls. A New*

Translation (San Francisco: HarperSanFrancisco, 1996).

8. Shanks, *Freeing the Dead Sea Scrolls*, 165.

9. Hector L. MacQueen, "The Scrolls and the Legal Definition of Authorship," in Lim and Collins, eds., *The Oxford Handbook of the Dead Sea Scrolls*, 723–48; Timothy Lim, Hector L. MacQueen, and Calum M. Carmichael, eds., *On Scrolls, Artefacts and Intellectual Property* (Sheffield: Sheffield Academic Press, 2001).

1Q/ 4Q etc.: Texts found in Cave 1/Cave 4 at Qumran

Alexander Jannaeus: High Priest and King, of Judea, 103–76 BCE

Antiochus Epiphanes: Syrian king, whose attempt to suppress the Jewish cult in Jerusalem led to the Maccabean revolt (168–164 BCE)

apocalypse/apocalyptic: Revelatory writings, dealing with the heavens and with the end of history.

Damascus Document: Text found in the Cairo Geniza in 1896, of which copies were found among the Scrolls. Describes a movement that formed a new covenant.

Enochic Judaism: A movement described in apocalyptic writings attributed to the patriarch Enoch, who supposedly lived in the seventh generation from Adam. Possible forerunner of the movement described in the Scrolls.

Eschatology: Discussion of the last things, both the end of history and death and the hereafter of individuals

Essenes: Jewish sect around the turn of the era. Thought to be the movement reflected in the Dead Sea Scrolls.

Gathas: Hymns of the Iranian prophet Zoroaster (Zarathustra)

Halakah: The Pharisaic and rabbinic term for religious law

Hasidim: Pious people who supported Judas Maccabee in the Maccabean Revolt. Possible forerunners of the Essenes and the Pharisees.

Hasmoneans: Dynasty of priest-kings descended from the Maccabees

Herod: King of Judea, 37–4 BCE.

Hodayot: Thanksgiving Hymns

Hyrcanus II: High Priest 76–67 BCE and 63–40 BCE

Josephus: Jewish historian, late first century CE

Jubilees: A variant account of Genesis and part of Exodus, supposedly revealed to Moses at Sinai

LXX: The Septuagint, or Greek translation of the Bible, so called because of a legend that the Torah was translated by 72 scribes

Manual of Discipline: The Community Rule found in Qumran Cave 1. Also called 1QS or Serek ha-Yaḥad.

Masoretic Text: The traditional text of the Hebrew Bible

MMT: Miqsat Maʿase ha-Torah. (Some of the Works of the Law). Text from Cave 4 outlining the reasons why the sect separated from the rest of Judaism.

MT: Masoretic Text. The traditional text of the Hebrew Bible.

Nabateans: Ancient people south and east of the Dead Sea

Nash Papyrus: Four fragments found in 1898, containing the Ten Commandments and the start of the prayer "Hear O Israel." Dates from 150 to 100 BCE. Oldest Hebrew manuscript fragment known before the discovery of the Dead Sea Scrolls.

Paleography: Study of ancient handwriting

Pesher/pesharim: Distinctive commentaries on prophets and psalms found in Dead Sea Scrolls

Pharisees: Major Jewish sect around the turn of the era. Viewed as opponents in the Dead Sea Scrolls.

Philo: Jewish philosopher in Alexandria, early first century CE

Pliny: Roman writer killed in eruption of Vesuvius in 79 CE

Plutarch: Greek writer and philosopher, 46–120 CE

Sadducees: Major Jewish party around the turn of the era. Sectarian law in the Scrolls agreed with that of the Sadducees in some cases.

Serek: Distinctive term for a "rule book" in the Scrolls

SP: The Samaritan Pentateuch

Temple Scroll: Long scroll acquired by Israelis in 1967. Combines texts from Leviticus and Deuteronomy in a new revelation.

War Scroll: Directions for final battle between Sons of Light and Sons of Darkness

Zoroastrianism: Ancient Iranian religion that posits two opposing spirits of light and darkness

BIBLIOGRAPHY

TRANSLATIONS

F. García Martínez, *The Dead Sea Scrolls Translated*
(Leiden: Brill / Grand Rapids, MI: Eerdmans,
1996).

G. Vermes, *The Complete Dead Sea Scrolls in English*
(London: Penguin, 2004).

M. Wise, M. Abegg, and E. Cook, *The Dead Sea Scrolls.
A New Translation* (San Francisco: HarperSan-
Francisco, 1996).

REFERENCE WORKS

L. H. Schiffman and J. C. VanderKam, eds., *Encyclopedia of the Dead Sea Scrolls* (2 vols.; Oxford: Oxford
University Press, 2000).

P. W. Flint and J. C. VanderKam, eds., *The Dead Sea
Scrolls after Fifty Years. A Comprehensive Assessment*
(2 vols.; Leiden: Brill, 1998).

T. H. Lim and J. J. Collins, eds., *The Oxford Handbook
of the Dead Sea Scrolls* (Oxford: Oxford University
Press, 2010).

THE SCROLLS AND THE MEDIA

M. L. Grossmann and C. M. Murphy, with the assistance of Allison Schofield, eds., *The Dead Sea Scrolls in the Popular Imagination*, = *Dead Sea Discoveries* 12/1(2005), especially the contributions by L. H. Schiffman, "Inverting Reality: The Dead Sea Scrolls in the Popular Media," (pp. 24–37), and G. J. Brooke, "The Scrolls in the British Media (1987–2002)," (pp. 38–51).

INDEX OF ANCIENT TEXTS

Maccabee, Simon, 75, 208
Magen, Yitzhak, 81, 83
Magness, Jodi, 73, 77, 79, 80, 82, 86, 95
Man of the Lie, 15, 204, 207
Mary, 111
Mason, Steve, 65
Menahem the Essene, 123
Meyers, Eric, 95
Michael, archangel, 149, 150
Michaelis, J. D., 42
Milik, Józef T., 17, 25, 31, 56, 75, 106, 109, 110, 112, 113, 214, 215
Miriam, 195
Mishnah, 239
Mittmann-Richert, Ulrike, 31
Moffett, William, 223
Mohammed ed-Dib, 4
Moses, 62
Murphy-O'Connor, Jerome, 159

Nabateans, 83
Najman, Hindy, 212
Nebuchadnezzar, 73
Nehemiah, 24, 25
Newman, Judith H., 212
Newsom, Carol, 177, 217

O'Callaghan, José, 137
Origen, 5
Oxtoby, Will, 19

Pardee, Dennis G, 241
Parthians, 76
Paul, Saint, 134, 135, 136
Paul, Shalom, 66
Peleg, Yuval, 81, 83
Pfann, Stephen J., 31, 68
Pharisees, 35, 43, 47, 50, 56, 57, 58, 152, 160, 161, 168, 170, 171, 178, 191, 192, 198, 202, 203
Philo, 33, 35, 37, 39, 40, 49, 50, 53, 61, 62, 63, 64, 172
Plato, 48
Pliny, 33, 35, 39, 52, 60, 64, 68, 89, 91, 92, 152
Pompey, 100, 204

Ptolemy II, 186
Protestants, 42, 47
Puech, Emile, 113, 221, 223, 230
Pythagoras, 38, 47, 48
Pythagoreans, 39, 47, 49, 51, 53, 62

Qimron, Elisha, 166, 216, 226, 229, 230–33

Rabin, Chaim, 56, 160
Ranke, Leopold von, 56
Renan, Ernest, 45–46, 99
Rengstorff, Karl-Heinrich, 23, 24, 31
Riesner, Rainer, 137
Robinson, James M., 225, 231
Rockefeller Foundation, 18
Rodgers, Zuleika, 65
Romans, 28, 77, 149, 182
Rossi, Azariah de, 43
Roth, Cecil, 56, 61

Sadducees, 35, 56, 57, 58, 168
Safire, William, 223
Salahi, Faidi, 5
Salome Alexandra, 179
Samaritans, 186, 191
Samuel, Mar, 2, 3, 5, 6, 8, 33
Sanders, James, 201, 202, 222
Sarah, 194
Scaliger, Joseph Justus, 42
Schechter, Solomon, 14, 30
Schiffman, Lawrence, 66, 165, 180, 182, 228, 234
Schuerer, Emil, 44
Schuller, Eileen, 65, 217
Shanks, Hershel, 217, 218, 221, 230–33, 239, 241
Shemesh, Aharon, 183, 184
Silberman, Neil Asher, 30, 34, 237, 241
Severus, 5
Skehan, Patrick W., 18, 106, 202, 213
Smith, Morton, 175

INDEX OF PLACES

INDEX OF SUBJECTS